'In *A Call Less Ordinary*, Rᵢ glorious adventure to which we are called is not always straightforward or easy, but it's definitely worth it. Rich shares hard-won lessons for anyone who aspires to be part of a movement that will influence a generation.'
Dr Roger Bretherton, clinical psychologist

'Rich encourages us with his voyage of discovery, exploration and adventure, but during it all, his faithfulness and the Father's faithfulness both shine through. This is a book for young and old alike.'
Martin Dyer, professor of oncology

'I would urge anyone, at any stage of "their race", to read this book either to begin their journey of discovery in their calling or to support them through their walk furthering God's kingdom.'
Emma, Royal Navy marine engineer officer

'*A Call Less Ordinary* brings alive ancient wisdom with stories, people and experiences that are distinctly modern and relevant.'
Graeme English, strategic projects manager

'I know I will pick it up and put it down going forward and will be challenged and inspired to live a life of purpose rooted in a deep relationship with God.'
Chris Ford, police officer

'Working through God's call in our lives can be a roller-coaster – this authentic and vulnerable account of that journey will inspire those who seek to serve the purposes of God in their own unique way.'
Richard Gamble, CEO, The Wall

'This book is packed with so much truth and heart – a story that leaves you reeling and awakened all at once. Rich brings it all to the table, reminding us to pursue community, adventure and obedience in our Christian walk . . . no matter where we are. I look forward to reading it again, again and again.'
Ruri Gicheha, singer-songwriter and PhD student

'Raw, honest and compelling – a timely and necessary message well lived and beautifully written for this generation.'
Pete Greig, 24-7 Prayer International and Emmaus Rd, UK

'Rich Wilson's vulnerable and raw account of his life and calling is both inspiring and humbling, and I found myself being drawn closer to God with each page, as I reflected on God's faithfulness and love in this imperfect world. The question of calling isn't just something for people in their twenties but is a daily question for us all. *A Call Less Ordinary* encourages us to embrace the adventure ahead of us, and I have definitely been inspired to that.'
Rebecca Halse, teacher

'Rich's story invites us into the hope and cost of embracing God's calling to adventure and risk as we pursue Jesus and his calling to seek first the kingdom. Rich's testimony helps us to navigate our own inner adventure with God, steering us

around the attitudes that get us stuck and lifting our eyes to the destination. He helps us to recognize the patterns in our life and strengthens our trust in the Father who guides us.'
James and Fjona Hill, hoteliers

'A warm and kind, yet powerful ushering to purpose, and away from passivity. An encouragement to take sturdy steps into the unknown. *A Call Less Ordinary* encourages us to feel the feelings and walk through the fires but to know you're never alone, and it is never in vain. This book called me to view my journey thus far, to be reminded that God always finds the rubies in the rubble, the diamonds amid the sooty coal.'
Anna Mathur, psychotherapist, writer and speaker

'This book is a wonderful reminder that our calling is so intrinsic to who we are. Rather than something to search for, it is a gift as abundant as breath itself, and waking up to that potential is a beautiful thing.'
Becca Nye, fashion designer

'This is a book that will encourage, challenge and excite readers anywhere on the scale between being fully confident in their calling and having no idea of what God is calling them into. It is written with a vulnerability and authenticity that allow the wisdom provided to go straight to the heart, showing how God can use every experience in our lives, and allowing the reader to walk into a life of greater freedom and purpose. I will be recommending this book to all my student friends!'
Tilly Picket, student

'I finished this book with a desire to put my pen down and stop trying to write my own life story. In the past few years, my desire for perfection has been crowding out my desire for adventure. And yet, some of the best parts of my life began as interruptions in my perfect plan. Rich reminded me that I don't want a life story I can imagine. I want something God-sized. I am praying that I have the stomach to handle God's adventure!'
Stefanie Reid MBE, athlete, speaker and broadcaster

'This book will stir your heart, open your eyes and wake you up to God's invitation for your life. To come and follow him on a much bigger adventure than you could ever imagine on your own. The stories and the hard-won life wisdom contained in these pages will move you: to tears, to hope, to prayer and to greater faith in the Author behind the writer of these words. Read it ready to respond, share it with your friends, place it like a lighter into the hands of young adults and pray for truth and life to ignite, sparks to fly and calling to be set on fire, for the sake of the world and the generation that is growing up in it. This is a call less ordinary, but it is one worth giving everything to respond to.'
Miriam Swanson, Global Student Mission Leader, Fusion

Rich Wilson is the leader of the Fusion movement and has pioneered pathways and resources for churches to work with students and student workers to be trained. He is part of the senior leadership team of Open Heaven Church in Loughborough, England. Home is shared with his wife Ness, their two daughters and often one or two others.

A CALL LESS ORDINARY

Why your purpose matters

Rich Wilson

First published in Great Britain in 2020

Society for Promoting Christian Knowledge
36 Causton Street
London SW1P 4ST
www.spck.org.uk

The author and publisher have made every effort to ensure that the external
website and email addresses included in this book are correct and up
to date at the time of going to press. The author and publisher are not
responsible for the content, quality or continuing accessibility of the sites.

Copyright acknowledgements can be found on page 217.

British Library Cataloguing-in-Publication Data
A catalogue record for this book is available from the British Library

ISBN 978–0–281–08188–2
eBook ISBN 978–0–281–08189–9

Typeset by Falcon Oast Graphic Art Ltd
First printed in Great Britain by Ashford Colour Press
Subsequently digitally printed in Great Britain

eBook by Falcon Oast Graphic Art Ltd

Produced on paper from sustainable forests

For Amelie and Lauren
and in loving memory of Josiah

Contents

Prologue

A vision

Generation after generation of students igniting fire after fire
in the lives of fellow students.
Multitudes seeing a vision for God's preferred future
and kneeling in submission to his kingdom cause.
Seeds of calling planted which, over time, would grow into
huge trees,
bearing fruit and providing shelter and home,
feeding both individual names and whole nations.
They are the peaceable freedom fighters and unlikely looking soldiers who lay down their lives for a fairer world.
They are the generous givers, unattached and unmoved by
the latest consumer craze, pouring out their resources for
an eternal Source.
Humbly and resolutely they take their stand.
Prophetically and mischievously their lives scream a better
way.
In the face of injustice, they make their demands,
giving voice to the voiceless and showing mercy to the
mistreated.
When they open their eyes, they see the world as God imagined,
through the brokenness and blood, the fingerprints of the
maker still evident on eight billion images.
Men and women, glorious shadows waiting for a divine
spark.

And when they open their mouths, declarations of grace pour forth:

shouting hope for the hopeless, healing for the hurting; God is much, much closer than you think.

And when they open up their stride, together they form a marching band,

a symphony of truth and wisdom,

a melody so attractive that culture can't help but dance to the beat.

Heaven's rhythm in heaven's people.

A stampede of God's children being unleashed into business, politics, church planting, education, arts, media, medicine and more.

Marked by encounter, they leave their mark in society for generations to come.

'Everyone will be forgotten, nothing we do will make any difference, and all good endeavours, even the best, will come to naught. Unless there is God. If the God of the Bible exists, and there is a True Reality beneath and behind this one, and this life is not the only life, then every good endeavour, even the simplest ones, pursued in response to God's calling, can matter forever.'

TIM KELLER, 'WHY CALLING MATTERS'

Introduction
Called by God?

I was driving along the outskirts of Loughborough when I saw my adult son for the first time. I had held him as a baby, just 24 hours old. Then no more. And yet here he was in front of me: a grown man of stature, a man who knew who and whose he was called to be. My son was dead, but as the Lord came close and the atmosphere in my car became thin, God was giving me just a glimpse into heaven's perspective on calling, one that would leave my life on earth forever changed. Death is not the end of the story. But this is not the start of mine. My story, like yours, begins in a garden . . .

A wide-open space. Full of beauty, purpose and potential. Teeming with life and creativity; *gloriously alive.* The first few chapters of the Bible give a short summary of where we have come from and why we are here. They sit at the beginning of a much larger narrative where, if you listen carefully, God can be heard in a multitude of different ways calling humanity, calling you: '*Ayeka*?' This short and profound word is the first question God asks in the Bible and it echoes through the whole of Scripture and into our lives today: 'Where are you?'

> '*God asks because we, humanity, need to hear the question, "Ayeka? Where are you in relation to me?"*'

When God first asks this question of Adam, he doesn't ask because he needs to know the answer. He is close by in the world he has created. The question isn't accompanied by heavy footfall causing the earth to tremble; it is a call that can be heard with a tremor of emotion within it: '*Ayeka*?' It is the call of a friend who feels deep longing and passionate concern, the call of a saviour who leaves the 99 and relentlessly pursues the one (Luke 15.4). This is the call of a good Father who stands, waits and gazes expectantly, longing for us to return home, eager to embrace us (Luke 15.20). '*Ayeka*?' Not 'Where are you physically?' This isn't a game of hide and seek. Not 'Where are you emotionally?' God already knows. This is a question about proximity: where are you in relation to me? God doesn't ask because he needs to know the answer. God asks because we, humanity, need to hear the question, '*Ayeka*? Where are you in relation to me?'

So, where are you? It may be that you know exactly where you are and precisely where you are going. The chances are, however, that the question of your 'calling' isn't quite so clear.

I have regular conversations with students and those in their twenties who are questioning life, longings and opportunities: is God calling me? To what? And where? And with whom? How do I navigate the next year, never mind the next decade? What is God's will for my life? How can I be confident that I am making the right decisions? What are the next steps? These far from being self-centred questions are very important – and they aren't confined to people who are leaving education behind. I have friends in their forties, fifties and sixties who know that God has more for them and that they have more to give. And yet, as we wrestle with these questions of calling, remember this: the initial call is the call to intimacy.

Over and above what you do or what you are to achieve in this life, at the core of your being you can know that God is passionately for you. We can have a close friendship with God because of close proximity. It is a crazy concept in our intellectually advanced culture. It is also a mysterious reality that millions of people declare makes them and completes them. From this place of intimacy with God we find identity, purpose and destiny.

This call to intimacy helps us better understand ourselves and the world around us. As well as caring deeply about where you are and how you are doing, God also has plans, dreams and assignments for you. They are bespoke, tailored and specific to you and the unique person he has made you to be. They may be different from what you expected, or they may happen with different timescales or in a different place from what you had in mind, but as you respond to God's call, '*Ayeka?*', he promises to show you the next step of the way. It is my prayer that, as you read this book, you will be convinced that God is passionate about you, that he loves you with an unending love and that he has plans to fulfil you, transform you and give you hope in all that life will throw at you.

This is a book where many stories collide. My story, your story and God's story. Like all good stories, they tell of adventure and adversity, heartache and hope, love and longings, risk and reward. They are about how I have wrestled with calling, been confused by it, humbled by it and tempted to give up on it, and also how I've treasured it, submitted to it and become profoundly grateful for it. As I have written these stories, God has challenged me to be more vulnerable than I would have chosen to be – sharing the painful and at times the ugly parts that don't get shared on social media, shared easily or shared at all.

My journey with calling hasn't always been easy, but it has never been taken alone: my story, like yours, is deeply connected to others. In many ways, the story of my calling is inextricably linked to the ups and downs of the Fusion movement which over the last couple of decades has seen thousands of students discover more of the call of God for their lives. Some stories have been written through tears and others are light-hearted but full of meaning; there are stories in which I am sure you will recognize yourself and perhaps identify with many of the challenges, emotions, questions, setbacks, dreams and desires experienced within them. They are stories about responding to the call of God that is there for each generation to grasp hold of and stories about following Jesus as a student: not just a three-year course but a lifelong quest to run the race marked out for us as well as we possibly can.

My prayer and hope are that these stories encourage you in your calling, transform your view of your significance and emphasize what an important role you have to play in this world and the plans and purposes of God. While it might not be recognizable at the moment, as you respond to the call of God, your life will also become a story that is worth telling.

'So Eli told Samuel, "Go and lie down, and if he calls you, say, 'Speak, LORD, for your servant is listening.'"'

1 Samuel 3.9

1

Calling and you: hearing the call

Dream big. These two words can prompt such different reactions. For some of us our dreams are alive and well and we do our best to chase them down. For others, these dreams seem hazy or hard to explain. For others still, these dreams have been shut down by fears, doubts and disappointments. Some might feel unable to dream or unable to trust their dreams.

The good news for those who follow Jesus is that we follow a God who dreams *for us*. A God who instals dreams within us that, because of the dreamer, will come about; dreams that awaken purpose and meaning; dreams that, as you respond to God's calling, you begin to find yourself participating in. Dreams that, like Samuel, we need to be awake to, no matter how or where they might begin.

I used to anticipate arriving at a place called 'calling', a place where everything would become clear, my life plan would be revealed and I'd know what I was for. Imagine my surprise, therefore, when my first 'ignition moment' – an encounter that would impress something of the call of God within me – took place on an understated farm near Norwich and seemed to have little impact on my life as I returned home. In a culture that tells us to 'dream big', we can overlook the seeds of calling that so often start small, and are usually planted in us from the beginning.

Back to the beginning

'Your childhood doesn't define you,
but God does, and he's been working
in you from day one.'

Whatever our upbringing, we can't escape the fact that our childhood shapes us. The lessons learned in these early years are often hidden and subconscious, only to surface in later life. For many of us, they provide hints of our calling integrated into who God has made us to be. What's more, when we respond to God, he takes all our days – the good ones, the bad ones and the ugly ones – and covers them with his grace, declaring, 'I can use this!' as he calls you forward. Your childhood doesn't define you, but God does, and he's been working in you from day one.

My own story begins in a small village about ten miles outside Manchester. I had lots to be thankful for: a loving and supportive family, a good network of friends and lots of opportunities to play sport – a pursuit that made me feel fully alive. I was also brought up to go to church from a young age. Though this is something I am now very grateful for, in my teenage years this was often not my attitude. Despite having a strong belief in God, I struggled to understand the relevance of the Church. I felt disillusioned, frustrated and agitated by the church meetings and, in a life stage where I needed role models and spiritual fathers, I didn't recognize any in my church.

As the time neared to leave home for university, two changes were happening in me. The first was that I longed for a new adventure and was feeling increasingly fidgety. The second was a deeper spiritual hunger: while my desire for church was still lacklustre, my passion for God was growing. I'd had a spiritual encounter as a child and one in my early teens, and another would form part of my preparation for university in the most unlikely of settings.

A Pentecostal farmer

A farm near Norwich seemed a strange place to go for a youth weekend away. Surely there was somewhere we could have stayed that didn't demand a 400-mile round trip? As is often the case with God's economy, it isn't about the place, the cost or the distance; it is about the people. Tony and Jean Gardiner were the people who were hosting us and teaching us about life in the Spirit. Tony – a fiery Pentecostal farmer who sounded as if he'd been mentored by the Old Testament prophet Elijah – told story after story in his broad Norfolk accent of signs and wonders, and how his own life had been radically saved by the grace of God. As a 17-year-old I lapped them up, his stories of his God encounters replenishing and reassuring my real-but-dry faith. I knew there had to be more, and there in Norfolk I was discovering some of what I longed for, which, even though I didn't have the language or theology to name it at the time, was the Holy Spirit.

On the Sunday afternoon, I went to ask Tony a question in his lounge. I have no recollection of the question or whether it was answered. I do remember that, as I stood there, he prayed for me and I began to sob uncontrollably: this would be my ignition moment. Nothing dramatic changed – my life was still largely enjoyable, uneventful and ordinary. But something small and subtle had started to stir: I began to hear God calling me: 'Ayeka?'

I started to recognize God's voice and be aware of his presence more: not just every few months or on Sundays, but daily, even hourly. The penny slowly dropped that following Jesus really was about putting him and his kingdom first. The deepest parts of me began to yearn for deeper connection with God, my desire and appetite for him changing. It is a desire and an appetite I am still working out almost three decades later, but it was as if in that moment I had been assigned a quest in life. I didn't know what that was, but I knew it was real. I had a new longing for God, and that in itself was the adventure. Into an ordinary 17-year-old living an ordinary life came the growing call of an extraordinary God.

God calls the ordinary

I imagine that, like many of us, at the time of this encounter I definitely shared the description Paul paints in his letter to the Corinthians: 'Remember, dear brothers and sisters, that few of you were wise in the world's eyes or powerful or wealthy when God called you' (1 Corinthians 1.26, NLT).

The great news is that calling often comes to ordinary people in ordinary places. Adam wasn't the only one we read of in the Bible who was hiding from something. Gideon hides in a winepress (Judges 6.11); Moses hides in a desert (Exodus 3.1); Elijah hides in a cave (1 Kings 19.9). Others are getting on with their lives: Samuel is sleeping (1 Samuel 3.3); Rahab is selling sex (Joshua 2.1); Jochebed is a new mum (Exodus 2.7); David is watching sheep (1 Samuel 16.11); Peter is fishing (Luke 5.4); Paul is on a killing spree (Acts 9.1). Not many were of high standing: Esther was an orphan (Esther 2.7); Rahab a prostitute (Joshua 2.1); Mary a teenage peasant (Luke 1.48). The inclusive call of God meant that they all found themselves included in God's plans.

> *'The great news is that calling often comes to ordinary people in ordinary places.'*

It doesn't matter what you have done or where you are now; what matters is that God is calling you. He is calling you in all your ordinariness, your boredom, your sin, your brokenness. You may feel unnoticed, but God's calling means he has noticed you and sees more in you than you dare to believe.

If, like me, you are prone to doubt, you are in good company. Doubting we have what it takes almost seems like a qualifying attribute. We need God to outwork our calling. It is, after all, a partnership. However, that doesn't stop the tried and tested excuses being used time and again; Gideon protested, 'I am the youngest' (Judges 6.15, NET), Moses lamented, 'I am slow of speech and slow of tongue' (Exodus 4.10) and Jeremiah borrowed both excuses as he remonstrated, 'I can't speak for you! I'm too young!' (Jeremiah 1.6, NLT). Sarah laughed off the call because of her old age (Genesis 18.12).

We could add any number of other excuses: I can't afford it; it's too hard; I don't know where to start; I am scared of failing; my parents won't approve; I haven't got what it takes. We convince ourselves that these are reasonable, rational, thought through and valid; however, when it is God who is doing the calling, our best excuse isn't good enough. Don't believe the lies and don't be tempted to make excuses. God knows you. He knows your desires and doubts; he sees your weakness and potential. He calls you right where you are, as you are, and promises to guide and shape you. He takes your ordinary life and transforms it with divine calling.

A defining time

My experience with the Pentecostal farmer happened shortly before I was due to start university, and it wasn't long before my dad was dropping me off in the centre of the campus. Loughborough was my chosen destination, and although I hadn't made the grades, they'd let me in anyway. The first term was a whirlwind, providing few moments to catch my breath. While I was busy making new friends and settling in, I had no idea that living in this small market town in the heart of England would become a training ground for a much bigger God adventure.

My university years would become a defining time. If you are studying now, the choices you make about who to be friends with, what you do with your time and how you pursue God will begin to set a course for your life. Your direction matters. A few degrees out over a few weeks or months doesn't make much difference, but over years and decades you may end up drifting into a place you never wanted to be. Begin to chart your trajectory now.

I met people from different backgrounds, cultures and nations, and my education was much broader and at times much more interesting than the course I was studying. Amid all the new experiences that university offered, my appetite for God continued to grow. Following my encounter in Norfolk, I explored churches different from the Anglican tradition I had grown up in and I attended a Pentecostal church during my first year. It was familiar in focus and refreshingly different in style, but although I attended the meetings, I didn't really integrate into the church community; not many students did in those days.

I also ventured to a Christian Union meeting on campus. I don't remember the meeting, but I do remember an attractive blonde student standing up on a chair and inviting everyone to go clubbing in town to celebrate her twenty-first birthday. Her name was Ness. At that time, I had absolutely no inkling how our paths would collide to form the deepest of friendships and one of the most exhilarating God adventures as our lives would become bound together in marriage. It wasn't love at first sight and I didn't fancy her, but I was *attracted* to her: she was full of energy, enthusiasm and passion for Jesus. We quickly became good friends, but it would be a few years before my romantic feelings for her would take me by surprise.

My growing curiosity towards God, people and the world led me to try some new things. I started a meeting at 7 a.m. every Monday morning to pray for the nations. To my bewilderment, often 40 to 50 people would show up. Prayer would fuel an inner fire that began to be expressed in activities and trips requiring adventurous faith. I teamed up with university pals Simon Guillebaud, Russ Smith and Craig Riley to go on a four-week mission trip to Brazil at the end of my first year. The following summer I went on my own to join a mission base in Israel where I lived on Mount Carmel for three months. I longed to be used by God, and these trips were expressions and explorations of my calling.

Exploring your calling

University gave some of the callings that were stirring in me space to breathe. I always thought discovering my calling was an 'event' in the future where I would feel different about life and be doing things that were significant in the eyes of others. It hadn't occurred to me that from the moment I set my heart, mind and strength on following Jesus I was starting to outwork my calling. It mattered less what I was doing and more who I was becoming; it mattered less what I did and more how I did it. I was already on the road where calling is outworked, winding through the hills and valleys and occasionally all the way to the mountaintops: it is not about arriving, but about allowing yourself to journey and explore.

Self-discovery takes time, and you may need to give yourself a break and be kinder to yourself as you wrestle with longings whose times haven't yet come. This is the paradox of calling: you are called fully and completely today and at the same time God's calling grows in you and shapes how you live moving forward. When was the last time you made a decision to go somewhere new or acted on an instinct? Are there places you need to visit? Are there people you need to pursue and hang out with? I wonder what things you might discover and learn and what new opportunities may result if you were to allow yourself the space.

> 'Self-discovery takes time, and you may need
> to give yourself a break and be kinder to
> yourself as you wrestle with longings whose
> times haven't yet come.'

Open Heaven

I touched down from Israel less than 24 hours before my final year at university began. To say I was experiencing culture shock would be an understatement, and my recent independence had me questioning, *Do I really need to commit deeply to a church? I'm only going to be here for another eight months.* Thankfully, my friend Giles challenged me to ask God for his perspective. God's answer was clear and came as an inner conviction, something I knew I had to do.

I connected with an unlikely bunch of people who were planting a church called Open Heaven. I'd never been to a meeting, so it wasn't a decision based on what I might get out of it. It was a response to God. I phoned Giles and said, 'I'm in; I'm committed.'

Open Heaven wasn't a meeting or a building or a brand; it was just a small group of seven ordinary graduates who were passionate about God – Giles, Mac, Kev, Rach, Brian, Lynda and Ness. I realized then that church is people joining in with the mission of God, and for the first time in my life church felt incredibly exciting. It was raw, experimental and authentic – a group of people who loved Jesus and were prepared to step out and pioneer for him. God was attracted to them and I was attracted to them. There was nothing on the surface that was particularly impressive, but their passion and their heart after God were contagious. I was hooked.

Passionate pursuit

Like Open Heaven itself, calling in these early years felt raw and authentic; it was experimental and I made mistakes. So often we think we need to 'find' our calling in order to begin, but, as we have seen, calling is something that is within us from the beginning and that God wants to call out of us more and more as he puts new hopes and dreams into our hearts.

Encouraged by people around me who were passionate for God, I remember us chasing his presence around the country as a great outpouring of the Spirit – dubbed the 'Toronto Blessing' owing to its origins in a small church in Canada in 1994 – spread around the world. We drove as far north as Newcastle and down to London and the south coast of England to be part of these meetings and to connect with God. I fully believe you can connect with God precisely where you are, but I also believe God responds to our hunger when it comes to discovering more of our calling. Though our calling is planted within us, a greater sense of understanding and purpose won't happen without passionate pursuit of God.

How much do you want to discover more of your calling, and to what lengths are you prepared to go? It is about much more than meetings; it is about a spiritual self-awareness that recognizes those yearnings for more and refuses to ignore them. It is about a posture that accepts the ordinariness of the present and declares, 'Lord, start here, where I am and as I am,' knowing that God will respond, 'Let's begin.'

'For everything there
is a season,
a time for every activity
under heaven.'

ECCLESIASTES 3.1 (NLT)

2

Calling and character: longings and seasons

University was fast drawing to a close. The clear path of education that had been so easy to follow was coming to an abrupt halt, and uncharted territory lay ahead. Like me, you may have imagined being more energized by the new world of possibility, but when it arrives it can feel threatening. Looking ahead to the great unknown, only one question remained: 'What next?'

Maybe you are asking that question right now. Maybe you've been asking it for a while. And if you're not asking it, it is likely that this well-meaning question is coming at you from all sides: from friends, parents, parents of friends and friends of parents. 'What's next?' is a courageous question, but it can also provoke feelings of displacement and confusion: Where do I go? Am I stuck? Shouldn't I be moving forward by now?

Learning to wait

It was around this time that I felt God reveal to me the prophetic vision found in the prologue of this book: *Generation after generation of students igniting fire after fire in the lives of fellow students.* In an ordinary moment, while I was reading alone in the community house I was living in shortly after graduation, I became aware of God's calling growing in me. There was no angel, no audible voice, no burning bush; just a sense within my being that I had something more to offer students. It was like being on a mountaintop on a cloudless day.

Calling can have these great moments of clarity, but I find they are rare. More often we need time and space to recognize the thoughts and questions God is stirring in our hearts. Even after this 'mountaintop' moment, I found myself back in the valley of waiting and confusion as I was learning that cultivating calling takes a great amount of patience and a willingness to let our longings grow and take shape.

It was on an October afternoon, while I was sitting in a fireside chair, that God revealed more of the call he had placed on my life. Though the mountaintop experience didn't last long, and everyday life began again, I felt different. I'd touched something that I couldn't unhear, unsee or ignore. It had become etched in my mind's eye, as though I had looked for a fraction of a second too long at the sun, and even though my eyes were turned away or shut tight, the heat spot still remained in my vision. I knew in that moment that my big questions, such as, 'What would it take to disciple a whole generation of students?', weren't just my questions; these were seeds that God had planted in me and was encouraging to grow.

You might be able to identify with similar 'sticky thoughts' – questions and dreams that refuse to let go and keep hanging around, inviting you to muse on them. Have you noticed them? Have you written them down or uttered them out loud? Who could comprehend the ideas and callings that start with a small thought? Capturing these moments of clarity is important. These lingering impressions are so vital if we are to persevere into more and, as we shall explore, calling tends to be incubated in ordinary places, tested in dark places and realized in unlikely places. This by its very nature means we must learn how to 'wait'.

'You might be able to identify with similar
"sticky thoughts" – questions and dreams that
refuse to let go and keep hanging around,
inviting you to muse on them.'

'Wait, Israel, for GOD. Wait with hope. Hope now; hope always!' sing the pilgrims in Psalm 131.3 (MSG) as they embark on the long and arduous journey to Jerusalem. It is not easy to wait – to wait our turn, to wait in life, to watch others go ahead of us while we are still waiting – when at the same time we are sensing that there is so much more in us, more for us and we have more to offer. Pride tries to make things happen; humility waits. Humility trusts God; humility requires faith that if we don't push ourselves forward, God will release us in his time and in his way.

This sort of waiting is far from passive; it is often charged with frustration and longing. But in it we discover more of our identity and calling. Waiting is transformative. In the hiddenness and surrender, God is working for our good. Peter writes, 'Humble yourselves, therefore, under God's mighty hand, that he may lift you up in due time. Cast all your anxiety on him because he cares for you' (1 Peter 5.6–7). As part of our journey, Psalm 131 can become a chant, as we join in with the declarations of pilgrims who have gone before us. As we live in the tension, we wait for God, his timing, his green light, and we wait with hope – hope now; hope always! And if we dare to keep waiting, the destination we thought was on the other side, at the end of the journey, is in reality right beside us: God with us, alongside us and for us.

My own waiting would give birth to many questions that I am sure you can identify with, and while I couldn't articulate them at the time, my questions were around identity: Where is my worth? Am I lovable? How can I make a difference? What does it mean for me to be me? Why does this feel so hard? I was frustrated, really frustrated. Inside me was a longing to be significant, to make my contribution, to be noticed – especially by men and women I looked up to as role models. I wanted validation and affirmation.

All this was different from what I actually needed. God knew what I needed, and on his training programme I wasn't going to be given any false comforts, early promotions or trophies just for turning up. I wasn't going to get cheat sheets or shortcuts. As Paul reminded the Corinthian church, I also needed to be reminded: 'And don't be wishing you were someplace else or with someone else. Where you are right now is God's place for you' (1 Corinthians 7.17, MSG). You might need to stop and allow this verse to sink in.

Our response to these seasons of waiting is to make decisions that are faithful, to the best of our ability. Often that is doing what is in front of us. That is what I tried to do when that inevitable question started to rise again: 'What's next?'

What's in front of you?

I graduated from Loughborough University and decided to stay around to journey with the people I had been doing life with for the last couple of years (at Open Heaven and before that). This was my community – a couple of dozen people who were exploring what building church in student culture looked like. Externally there was nothing that would draw you in, except that, when we met, there was a sense of the presence of God that would invade our meetings, whether they were in homes, on campus or in an old, dilapidated wooden scout hut. With no great draw to move or 'go' elsewhere, I committed to what was in front of me: a year of training and serving this bunch of unlikely, adventurous and passionate Jesus-followers. It would also prove to be the start of the most challenging and formative season of my life so far, one where God took the opportunity to prepare me for things that I wouldn't understand until much later on.

I know my journey of wrestling with waiting is typical of so many new graduates. Full of potential and with a sense of God's hand on my life, I had a desire to be significant for God but didn't know which way to turn. If this is where you are right now, what is God teaching you? I was learning that what is important in the next step is not about landing the dream job, or even being fulfilled and realizing your potential. It is more about attitude – willingness to learn, to try new things and to give your best. It is about trusting that God will use your work and circumstances for his training and transformation in your life, and that his timing for the good works he has prepared for you to do is perfect.

Character and identity

As heady as my vision for students in my moment of clarity was, looking back I realize it was rooted in what I was already doing. I was already involved in student work, part of a student-focused church and spending most of my time with students – and I was loving it! God's calling in that moment was building on things that were already in my heart and giving me life. It was an encouragement to keep doing what I was doing knowing that God had more for me.

Much of what God asks of you is already in you. What are you passionate about? When do you feel most alive? What are you good at? The call of God is designed to resonate with who you are, and one of the reasons it sometimes feels unclear is that true identity, rather than labels, is something that is still being discovered. Identity in Christ and understanding ourselves takes time. So much of the potential we carry and feel hasn't been expressed yet. We need to be patient and kind to ourselves in the waiting.

Even if we feel we have embraced our true identity, calling almost always involves stepping outside our comfort zone and into some big unknowns. God's calling on our lives is always for something bigger than ourselves. To engage with deeper aspects of calling requires us to be self-forgetful – less concerned with ourselves and more concerned with God. We can be sure that when we have frustrations and longings that go beyond ourselves, it means that aspects of calling are being incubated and discovered.

'Calling almost always involves stepping
outside our comfort zone and into some big

unknowns. God's calling on our lives is always
for something bigger than ourselves.'

What can be both reassuring and overwhelming at the same time is that God calls us personally by name (Isaiah 43.1; John 10.3). It is reassuring because our future in God is mapped out for us. It is overwhelming because we don't get a copy of the map! God's call is an invitation to trust. In the day to day, God promises to be a lamp to our feet and a light to our path (Psalm 119.105). God is in the light, and he is also in the darkness (see Psalm 97.2). In God's wisdom and in our best interests, he asks us to trust him with the next step and with what lies ahead.

God in all seasons

Trusting God while trying to discern greater clarity around calling can be hard. After my God-charged daydream I found my external circumstances hadn't changed, but something inside me had. When I roused myself from that fireside chair it felt as though I was ejected into a spiritual winter. Though I didn't have the language for this at the time, I have since come to view this season of life (and many more that were to come) as a personal 'wilderness'. I had little idea then that the wilderness can be a landscape for training and transformation, and that using the metaphor of seasons to help recognize the time of life we are in can be really helpful as we seek to follow God and outwork what he has called us to be and to do.

Summer. Summer demonstrates heaven on earth. It is warm, abundant, fragrant and alive with colour and new life. Summer is good and feels good. It has been said that character is often formed in failure and tested in success, and so summer carries a note of caution for us if we are in danger of getting too carried away with the good times. It can be harder to pursue God with the same intensity from a place of feeling strong. It may well be that it was the prayers and previous feelings of weakness, frustration and hunger that produced such an abundant summer.

Autumn. Autumn declares a beautiful and dignified death. Nature puts on a show with tremendous confidence, a liberal scattering of seed, a celebration of all that has gone before. Autumn is good although it feels threatening. It signifies the end of some things – closure. It challenges our identity when we have to move forward without these things. How will we let go? How will we plant our seeds? Autumn teaches us to recklessly abandon to God the things we can't control, and to do so joyously and without fear. God often stirs and provokes new aspects of calling in our spiritual autumns.

Winter. Winter hides treasures in the darkness. Cold and grey, damp and depressing and with short days and long nights, winter forces us to examine life more closely. Winter is good although it feels hard. Winter is the most transformative season: the seeds that go into the ground dormant with eyes of faith begin to birth new life. Hope is hidden but very much alive. Parker Palmer talks about our inward winters taking many forms – failure, betrayal, depressions, death:

> The winters will drive you crazy unless you learn to get out into them. Until we enter boldly into the fears we

want to avoid, those fears will dominate our lives. But when we walk directly into them protected from frost-bite by the warm garb of friendship or inner discipline or spiritual guidance – we can learn what they have to teach us.[1]

Spring. Spring takes fragile hope seriously. Stirring below the dirt are green shoots of potential. It isn't always evident what they will become, but become they will. New trees, flowers and shrubs all start somewhere, very small. Spring is good and dares to hope. As winter gives way to spring the days lengthen and light up new possibilities. God resurrects dreams that have been long since buried, some for 20, 30 or even 40 years.

A time for everything

Each season can offer a picture of what may be going on spir-itually in our lives. Whatever season you are in right now, you can be sure that God is with you, has good things for you and wants to give you his perspective. Unlike nature's sea-sons, these spiritual seasons don't always transition smoothly from one to another. We experience abrupt and traumatic season changes in our lives, and with each new season we receive a new set of questions to confront and wrestle with. Sometimes we can't see the seasons changing; at other times we are fully aware that we are seeing one season break into another – but in every season God calls us to himself, and there are opportunities for growth and transformation.

The years following my graduation were the hardest of my life up to that point, and what made it all the harder was that it was all hidden. On the surface there was nothing to suggest life was hard: there was no illness, grief, betrayal or broken dream. Below the surface it felt as though God was doing some major heart surgery. He is committed to my best and my best required transformation at a heart level: inside me were deep longings that had been awoken and whose time had not yet come. The winter wilderness did not provide the abundance I was looking for; it was dry and barren. The most profound spiritual life lesson was taking place, only I couldn't see it. God was forming my identity in him, above everything else; that is what he is most interested in. If I never amounted to anything, I would always be loved and held by God. I could do all sorts of things for him and contribute everything to his kingdom's cause, but only one thing matters: 'Ayeka?' Where am I in relation to him? How close do I dare journey?

Laying down dreams

The reality was that I was already outworking God's calling; it just didn't feel like what I'd heard or imagined. Zechariah 4.10 (NLT) commands: 'Do not despise these small beginnings, for the LORD rejoices to see the work begin.' The exit of this particular winter season for me would involve laying down the very dream that I believed God had placed in my heart.

> 'Zechariah 4.10 (NLT) commands: "Do not despise these small beginnings, for the LORD rejoices to see the work begin."'

My dream was a grain of wheat that needed to be planted. It wasn't just about hidden longings now; it was about killing them altogether and surrendering to God all I had been wrestling with and praying towards in the previous two and a half years. I wish I'd worked it out sooner, but I didn't. I surrendered in prayer and remember saying to God, 'You know best, and I will still love you and live for you whatever I do with my life.' I also acted out my surrender by taking a full-time job with a bank. It felt like failure.

I wasn't angry with God and I didn't want to throw the seed away in a tantrum, but I was confused. Jesus announced that unless a kernel of wheat falls to the ground and dies, it remains only a single seed. But if it dies, it produces many seeds (John 12.24). This was an allegory for Jesus' death and resurrection but also an invitation for me to willingly participate in his life. We can trust to God what belongs to him and be confident that he can resurrect what we bury. I think this is true of any specific calling in God – that it will be tested, and that calling is not cheap but costly. To be fit and ready to outwork more of God's call on our lives we willingly have to join the psalmist in saying, 'Test me, Lord, and try me, examine my heart and my mind' (Psalm 26.2). The testing is all about our heart and about preparation for partnering with God in his mission to the world.

Summer breaks in

It was during this difficult season that significant relationships started to make themselves known. The most significant of these was with Ness. We had become good friends over the previous three years, with many friends cheekily enquiring whether I 'liked her'. My answer was always the same: I did like her as my friend, nothing more. That was until what felt like a bolt from the blue disrupted my emotions as I began to fall in love with her. This came as a shock to me and I was a little frustrated by the feelings I was having towards her. I was really content in my singleness and, while I did want to get married sometime in the future, I didn't want a relationship then, and I certainly didn't want the feelings that were consuming me! I was looking forward to at least a year of singleness and being undistracted in this year that I was setting aside for God.

One of the big lies in society is that we need an exclusive relationship in order to be complete, and one of the great liberating truths in Scripture is that a marriage partner does not complete us – only God completes us. It is far better to stay single than date or marry someone who isn't running after God at the same speed as you. But for me, a switch had been flicked in me that I couldn't find an off button for; I was deeply attracted to Ness and her passion for Jesus: we were both pursuing God with everything we had and we discovered we were running at the same speed.

'One of the big lies in society is that we need an exclusive relationship in order to be complete, and one of the great liberating truths in Scripture is that a marriage partner does not complete us – only God completes us.'

We can't control who we fall in love with, but we can choose who we are going to marry. After lots of wrestling in prayer we joyfully acknowledged that God had drawn us together and that that was part of the call of God on our lives.

God is committed to giving us more of what we need, not necessarily more of what we want. When I fell head over heels in love with Ness, I was definitely given both! We married on the Loughborough University campus during the spring term. For us it was the obvious place to get hitched. We were committed to each other and we shared God's call to lead a church that students wanted to be part of. Summer had broken in while winter was still ongoing; the uncertainty of autumn was all around, while on 14 March it was undeniably spring. The 1980s band Crowded House provided the anthem for that time, and, like the British weather, we were experiencing four seasons in one day.

'They objected to him as a dangerous firebrand.'

DOROTHY SAYERS

3

Calling and community: dangerous firebrands

My relationship with Ness wasn't the only significant one that was cemented in my post-uni days. I had been drawn to Roger Ellis as a teenager when I first heard him speaking at a Christian event called Spring Harvest. He led Revelation Church on the South Coast. Roger spoke with passion and enthusiasm in a gruff, gravelly voice caused by too many heavy metal concerts in his younger days, and he had an adventurous spirit that I found contagious. It wasn't until many years later, however, that Roger noticed me.

During my training year with Open Heaven, I travelled to another meeting where Roger was speaking. I was near the back of the venue but I felt he had clocked me. Sure enough, when the ministry time started, Roger made a beeline towards me. I was a 21-year-old man, but as he prayed and prophesied he was calling out the father in me, speaking to the things God had ordained but of which I was unaware. Those words went to the core of my being, words that didn't make sense in my head but which my spirit resonated with and responded to.

This was a profound and emotional encounter that would define some of the deepest parts of my identity and remind me afresh that when we are called, we are called in the context of community: through significant people and groups that God wants us to journey with. And when he invites us, he invites us to join with the community of believers who have gone before.

Called together

Back in Loughborough, I reflected on my connection with Roger. In a church of young students and recent graduates I was longing for more spiritual fathering and began to pray for an opportunity to be mentored and discipled by him. Praying with boldness, I even prayed about working alongside Roger – not exactly practical given we lived more than three hours apart. And yet, God was orchestrating connections behind the scenes.

It was two and a half years after my tear-filled prayer time with Roger that Ness and I had lunch with him at a conference. He was excited to share a proposition with me. A new student movement had been launched six months previously. Its name was Fusion and, as you already know, it was about to become a big part of my story.

Over lunch, Roger explained how he wanted me to be involved in helping to establish student-led small groups around the UK that were centred on Jesus and reached out to their friends. This should have come as welcome news, given all I had felt God stirring in me, but I needed time to reflect. As is so often the case, the timing was off (well, my timing at least) and, as obvious as the decision appeared to Ness, I needed to pray about it. This was the conversation I'd wanted to have at least 12 months earlier. In my impatience I'd lost track of God's timing, but he continued to track with me. As I prayed, the daydreams for what could be began to flood back with greater intensity than before. The thought of working with Roger to pioneer a new student movement started to fill me with immense excitement, and so, six months later, I became Fusion's first full-time student worker.

We made an unlikely duo – Roger who had never been to university and me who had only just made it to university – but thankfully God was stirring something bigger than both of us at the grass roots of student culture. God was assembling an unlikely group of students and leaders to pioneer new models of mission and to unleash fresh creativity into this growing and diverse mission field, all the while with community at its core.

Community incubates calling

Who is your community? Maybe you can answer that question easily: a specific set of friends, your family or a group in your church. For others, you may find answering that question much harder or even painful, especially if you currently feel isolated or that there's no one else who shares your passions. I've never met anyone who hasn't felt lonely or misunderstood at some point in life. In the age of social media and a culture that celebrates being liked by a multitude of acquaintances, it can be easy to mistake followers for friends. But God, who lives in community as Father, Son and Spirit, has hardwired us to be intimately known and has designed us to work out our calling in community. Close friends are often able to see the unique contribution we can make more clearly than we do, and it's in small communities of believers where we can outwork Jesus' two greatest commandments to love God and love our neighbour.

> 'In the age of social media and a culture
> that celebrates being liked by a multitude
> of acquaintances, it can be easy to mistake
> followers for friends.'

No matter where you are right now, I would encourage you to pursue a church community that provides opportunities to know a smaller group of people on a more intimate level. Small groups, home groups, connect groups or hubs – no matter what they are called, community with Jesus at the centre is attractive and provides additional scaffolding and foundations for our calling in God. Calling is developed through many small decisions that prioritize following Jesus, and we need the help of friends to do that. We are not designed for individual pursuit of holiness. The holiness that God has for us is personal, corporate and social, and that means we find tremendous freedom in being with friends where we can be fearlessly honest, daringly vulnerable and ruthlessly accountable. Your calling and mine were never meant to be worked out alone, and in the early days of Fusion I learned a lot about this from my good friend Jono.

The community Jono built

When students arrive at university with their identity secure in God, they stand out. Not only was Jono West deeply committed to his journey of discipleship, he was also six foot four and had sun-bleached dreadlocks – so he *really* stood out. Jono was a community builder and one of many natural leaders whom God was raising up to be part of this new movement of small groups on fire for God and summoning students to pursue God's call.

Jono moved from just north of London to study at Sheffield University and would connect with a small, unconventional church and an even more unconventional church leader with a big heart and a way with words. His name was Baz and his introduction to Jono was, 'I hate southerners and I hate students.' They would become great friends.

Jono was disappointed by what he saw in some of the Christians at university – dry Bible study, holy huddles or complete conformity to a student culture with no boundaries.

Calling is often deepened and ignited through disappointment and frustration, and it was a catalyst for Jono to do something. Longing for authentic community, Jono started a small group, and using the Fusion Bible notes the group explored what building Jesus-centred community looked like. Soon one Fusion small group multiplied into two.

The idea was simple. It didn't need money, a building, a charity; it just needed a few enthusiastic Jesus followers. Breaking the mould of how students engaged with God's mission to the campus, Jono would meet to coach new small-group leaders in Bar One in the Sheffield Student Union building, and he would later lead a pilgrimage to the very first Fusion conference on the south coast of England – 18 students piling into cars and driving through the night, sleeping on a church floor, the heating broken and the temperature outside at minus five. Shunning comfort and embracing inconvenience, this was a group of students who would see amazing things happen.

Jono was one of many students stepping into God's invitation to work out calling together. The small-group vision was taking off, and Roger and I were soon to meet another group of students seeing amazing things – this time in Cambridge. When Gabriel Smy set up the Revival Society with a couple of mates, he had no idea how it would affect the destinies of hundreds of other students. Weary of stale tradition and an uninspiring status quo, they set up small groups that sparked new hope in the University of Cambridge. Fusion small groups were multiplying fast, and at their peak more than 40 student small groups were meeting in the colleges of Cambridge. Students were becoming Christians – it was messy and beautiful. New life always is.

What did calling look like for Gabriel? It looked like having a go at building community, taking some risks and being prepared to be misunderstood.

Communities opposed

Though Jono and Gabriel partnered with God, their efforts were not without opposition. You may have already discovered that in pursuing God's calling you encounter difficulties and opposition. This can come from powers and politics in society and, sadly, all too often can come from Christians who have become too comfortable in the status quo of how 'things have always been'. Church history is littered with accounts of how some of the greatest and most vociferous opposition to moves of the Spirit comes from within the Church.

*'You may have already discovered that
in pursuing God's calling you encounter
difficulties and opposition.'*

A small but vocal minority would try to warn the students
Jono was investing in that what was happening was not from
God and that Jono was dangerous. They were partly right:
Jono was dangerous – the number of student small groups in
Sheffield would multiply to 56 at their peak, and for a three-
year period one person a week would become a Christian!
In a similar way, when Gabriel started the Revival Society,
there were some who were soon knocking on his door demanding an end to it, claiming it would bring disunity and
quoting Bible verses out of context. Gabriel and those who
gathered around him endured much criticism, but they kept
going in pursuit of what God was asking them to do.

Dorothy L. Sayers, writer and close friend of C. S. Lewis,
once observed that those who encountered Jesus first-hand
'thought him too dynamic to be safe'. She continued:

> It has been left for later generations to muffle up that
> shattering personality and surround him with an atmos-
> phere of tedium. We have very efficiently pared the
> claws of the Lion of Judah, certified him 'meek and mild,'
> and recommended him as a fitting household pet for pale
> curates and pious old ladies. To those who knew him, how-
> ever, he in no way suggested a milk-and-water person: they
> objected to him as a dangerous firebrand.[1]

Thankfully for Jono, Gabriel and anyone else pursuing
calling in the face of opposition, we have the blueprint of

Jesus' life and the stories of thousands of believers who have gone before to encourage us as they have sought to pursue calling the Jesus way.

Pay attention to the past

You are not meant to work out calling alone. However, being part of a community of believers today is only one side of the coin. The other is knowing that you are part of a much larger community of believers who have gone before you. This is something that became abundantly clear to me when listening to another Roger – Roger Forster – as he inspired 300 students at the second ever Fusion conference. The room was captivated as he recalled the lives of women and men who had been obedient to God's call:

> The current student scene is one of the most significant scenes in the country. It is people like yourselves who are going to see that change take place, perhaps more than any other section of the community. Those sorts of people are usually gathered out of society between the ages of 18 and 25. So, we want to learn something of our roots by looking at student ministry in church history and world history and what we can contribute to it today. If we don't learn from the lessons of the past, if we don't pick up principles of what has gone on in the past, we will make the same old mistakes again.[2]

My heart began to race as he recounted stories of ordinary people captivated by the call of our extraordinary God: they were everyday revivalists made up of abolitionists, politicians, business leaders, captains of industry, financiers, theologians and cultural movers and shakers. This wasn't just a history lesson; this was *our* history, the bloodline of the Church. Eugene Peterson says this:

> Without a cultivated memory we live hand to mouth on fad and novelty. But Christians don't sprint out of the starting blocks in each generation in a race for heaven. We are on a relay team. We have a heritage, a richly composed family history.[3]

This family history for student mission starts with John Wycliffe, a professor, theologian, reformer and Bible translator born nearly 700 years ago in the mid-1320s. Wycliffe had a vision for a biblically based community, which started an uprising that would go on to change the nation as his students went from village to village preaching Christ. This movement in part paved the way for the Protestant Reformation, where Martin Luther – a theology professor, composer, priest and recovering monk – would become so outraged at the teaching and practices of the established Church that he would nail his 95 theses to the wooden chapel door that served as a message board for university staff. It was one of the most prophetic and provocative acts in church history. Again, it was students who would take his teaching and ideas forward, and Luther, like Wycliffe, was greatly opposed.

*'It almost seems unthinkable that in these
university towns believers would die for
their faith, but martyrdom is not just an*

> *uncomfortable storyline in our family history;*
> *it is also a present-day reality for parts of the*
> *global Church. I wonder what price we are*
> *prepared to pay for our current convictions.'*

This started a ripple effect: in Cambridge, two notable men, Thomas Bliney and Myles Coverdale, began preaching salvation by faith through the streets of the town, knowing they were doing so on pain of death. In Oxford, bishops Hugh Latimer and Nicholas Ridley were tied to a stake for doing the same. With fire lapping at their ankles, Latimer exhorted Ridley with these words: 'Be of good comfort, Master Ridley, and play the man! We shall this day light such a candle, by God's grace, in England, as I trust shall never be put out.'[4] It almost seems unthinkable that in these university towns believers would die for their faith, but martyrdom is not just an uncomfortable storyline in our family history; it is also a present-day reality for parts of the global Church. I wonder what price we are prepared to pay for our current convictions.

A chain of calling

Exactly 200 years after Luther, in the same university, the seeds of a global mission were being sown again. In 1716 a teenager by the name of Nikolaus Ludwig von Zinzendorf enrolled in the University of Wittenberg. He had already started the Order of the Grain of Mustard Seed with four schoolfriends with a simple creed: 'None of us lives for himself'. This small group was completely devoted to Christ and to one another, based on a simple premise that is still upheld today: that you spend time in the presence of Jesus daily in order to have something to contribute in a changing world.[5]

A few years later, Zinzendorf visited an art gallery in Dusseldorf and was captivated by Domenico Fetti's famous painting *Ecce Homo* ('Behold, the man'). Below the painting of Christ on the cross, the inscription read, 'This have I done for thee; What hast thou done for me?' In that moment, Zinzendorf realized he loved Jesus but had yet to serve him, and he resolved to do whatever Jesus asked of him. This led to him sharing his family's wealth to offer asylum to many persecuted wanderers from Moravia and Bohemia (parts of the Czech Republic today) and permitting them to build the village of Herrnhut on a corner of his estate. The Holy Spirit fell on this Moravian community, who went on to clock the longest prayer chain in history – unbroken for 100 years. The Moravians sent out hundreds of missionaries and thousands more followed. The mustard seed became a great tree.

It would be thanks to a Moravian missionary called Peter Boehler that a small group of students in Oxford would see a wave of revival sweep across the UK and change hearts and habits. He invited a young man by the name of John Wesley to a meeting in London, where he would have an ignition moment and his heart would be 'strangely warmed'.[6] Wesley returned to his small group, where holy fire spread through the university and the nation.

Wesley became a familiar figure on horseback, travelling an astonishing quarter of a million miles around the UK. In his lifetime he preached 40,000 sermons. He was a superb organizer who impressively raised up 10,000 small-group leaders and a rigorous discipleship culture through the asking of questions that helped men and women pursue God's calling.

The family inheritance

By delving into our family history, we can begin to grasp our full inheritance as believers, and a central part of our calling is how we invest this inheritance. Inheritance is a word that can invoke a sense of getting what we haven't worked for. Entitlement. Like the story of the lost son (Luke 15.11–32), eager to live off his inheritance early and not appreciating its true worth. One generation pays a price, works hard, sacrifices and then passes on what has been won to the next generation.

> *'I pray we aren't the generation that settles for soft-rock Christian gatherings and posting the occasional Bible verse on social media, but ultimately misses out on the adventure God is inviting us into.'*

Those who inherit can either sit back and enjoy what they have been given or look to build on what has gone before, adding their own creativity, energy and enthusiasm to the task. From our family history we inherit the fruit of their labour and their prayers, and we have a responsibility to invest it wisely. What would the generations of long ago make of this one? What will the generations to come make of us? We are writing history, whether we like it or not. I pray we aren't the generation that settles for soft-rock Christian gatherings and posting the occasional Bible verse on social media, but ultimately misses out on the adventure God is inviting us into.

Seeking to realize more of this inheritance, Roger and I met with some leaders and students in an upstairs room in Oxford. Together we wondered whether all the significant history in this place had been made, or whether there could be more.

After we had shared our vision, the reaction was disappointing. One student wearily summarized, 'This is Oxford . . . it is steeped in tradition and nothing really changes here because of that.' But as we turned to prayer, the atmosphere changed, faith began to rise and suddenly there was a dramatic power cut. What was lacking in human-made electrical power was being more than compensated for in spiritual power. As the Holy Spirit began to fill the room, one student began shaking and declaring Psalm 24:

> Open up, ancient gates!
> Open up, ancient doors,
>   and let the King of glory enter.
> Who is the King of glory?
> The LORD, strong and mighty;
> the LORD, invincible in battle.
> Open up, ancient gates!
> Open up, ancient doors,
>   and let the King of glory enter.
> Who is the King of glory?
> The LORD of Heaven's Armies –
>   he is the King of glory.
> (Psalm 24.7–10, NLT)

John Bilson was one of the students in that memorable 'upper room' meeting and considers his student years at Oxford as a season where his calling was ignited. He told me, 'For loads of us it changed our lives. We were infected with a vision for the kingdom that wrecked us.' He and his wife Nom have since church planted in France and are still living with the same vision to 'change a generation'.

The students around that time were up for an adventure, and five of them started the first Fusion small group in Oxford. Within three years, 150 students were meeting in groups across Oxford University and Oxford Brookes. And they weren't alone. Across the nation, God was calling others into these powerful communities. In Edinburgh, a Nigerian student called Olu started two Fusion small groups, and within a year they multiplied from two to eleven, beginning to meet every other week in the function room in the back of a pub. In Birmingham, two young women – Hannah Bowring (née West) and Kiera Phyo (née Singlehurst) – both heard God independently tell them to 'go to Birmingham and start something new'. Sharing the same hall of residence corridor during their first week and recognizing the divine setup, they stayed up all night sharing God's plans: they started a Fusion small group, which soon multiplied into two and then into 16 by the time they graduated.

Commitment defines calling

What was true around the country was also true where Ness and I were leading Open Heaven in Loughborough. Community was helping people come to know their primary call as children of God and then to work out their own unique callings in the context of a safe and encouraging family of believers. Fusion small groups had multiplied and were now present in all 21 halls on campus, and we were celebrating the steady stream of new life as many students found Christ.

We were also blessed with our own new life as our daughter Amelie was born and reduced the average age of an already very young church even further. In having a baby, Ness and I needed to work out new ways of working together, releasing each other and adding the very important calling of parenthood to all that we were doing. Being called to be a father touched on some of the core parts of my identity and, far from calling being something 'out there', I am increasingly being defined by who I am becoming as a husband, father, friend and colleague.

Working alongside Roger and Jono for those few years was like a whirlwind. Fusion small groups were in more than 50 university cities and multiplying quickly, swelling to around 500. We had started well and had a sense of being part of God's movement, but we needed a different approach to continue growing sustainably. The decision to stop counting Fusion small groups and to focus solely on helping local churches work with students felt costly. An obvious measure of 'our success' was to be replaced by a more ambiguous 'helping churches grow with students'. However, we were simply recognizing what was already happening: behind many of the students, from Olu to Hannah and Kiera, was a local church cheering them on.

Gradually, Fusion small groups were absorbed into churches, and the age of local church student ministry was born. I was convinced that it was the right decision, but I was also very aware that we could be killing all the movement and momentum that had been generated. Letting go of what I'd helped to build was hard for me.

In pursuing calling, the Bible never promises that we'll be immune from loss and pain. In fact, it suggests we should expect it, but I couldn't anticipate the pain both Ness and I were about to journey through. Though we'd have the gift of community to centre us, things were about to get a whole lot harder.

'The darker the night,
the brighter the stars,
The deeper the grief,
the closer is God!'

FYODOR DOSTOYEVSKY

4

Calling and pain: a long, dark night

I have never experienced pain like it, before or since. My chest was physically aching, disrupted by the emotional anguish I was enduring. I felt numb to everything except this clanging groan inside. I was completely at odds with my surroundings. It was a beautiful summer's day; the weather was hot and the sea flat and calm. The kind of day that seems to come around once every few years in North Wales where I was on holiday with Ness and Amelie. Everything external was all that you could wish for on holiday, especially in North Wales, except that there was one person missing – my son.

Six months earlier, we were gearing up for Christmas and looking forward to the birth of our second child, a baby boy. Our minds raced with an added anticipation in the Advent season. In the season of waiting and wonder, we were wondering what he would be like and how our lives would change with him in them. Would he get on with his older sister? Would she get on with him? Would he look like me? Would he share my enthusiasm for the outdoors? Or sport? So many hopes and dreams for what the year ahead would hold.

Looking back, there were some signs that things were not quite right. However, doctors, midwives and mother's intuition gave no hints of what lay in store. Pain was about to flood our world and shape our calling in a lesson I never wanted to learn.

Fearing the worst

Having nurtured, carried and prayed for our son, Ness was taken into hospital a week before Christmas suffering some pain. The next day she gave birth to Josiah Samuel Wilson. Our baby boy was alive but clearly very poorly. The room quickly filled with doctors and frantic activity. Josiah was whisked away to the intensive care unit, and in the vacuum of tiredness and uncertainty we were left alone. It became eerily quiet. This was not what we had imagined or hoped for. It was the winter solstice, and for us it was the beginning of a long, dark night.

For the next four hours we stayed alone in the delivery room. We prayed, talked a little and waited fretfully for updates. There were long silences and we battled hard to still our racing minds. Ness was exhausted from giving birth and I was feeling totally powerless and fearing the worst. It was an emotionally agonizing situation we found ourselves in.

After what felt like a torturous few hours, we were finally given some updates from midwives and doctors that Josiah was very poorly with a heart defect. It was obvious by some of the language they were using that they were gently preparing us for a very difficult time. At the same time, we had hope that we would all get through this and Josiah would make a full recovery.

Finally, we were invited to leave the delivery room to meet him properly for the first time. He lay peacefully, ventilators assisting his breathing and all wired up with lots of tubes. That morning as I had driven to the hospital, I had listened to a song by Athlete called 'Wires' and had wondered if we would end up here.

The reality before our eyes was a shock and felt more threatening than I could have imagined. Josiah's condition was critical. He needed an immediate transfer from Leicester General Hospital to a specialist unit at Leicester Royal Infirmary, where the staff kindly arranged for us to have a bed in the ward nearby. We drove across at 7 p.m. and had to wait another four hours before we could see him again. He was still very poorly but only needed 30 per cent oxygen as opposed to the 100 per cent he had needed before the transfer. There was a glimmer of hope for healing as the consultant said he'd 'fixed himself a bit' on the transfer.

Leaning into friendship

We updated friends and family with texts as concern for Josiah intensified around us. Our good friend Steve Clifford called and offered to come up from London to Leicester. We didn't know what we wanted or how to respond: some decision-making faculties were completely numb and others overloaded with thoughts and questions. We were plunged into huge uncertainty: Would he die? How long can he live? Would we be in and out of hospital for the next two years? Longer? If he lived would there be brain injuries? What would that mean? Oh, God, help. Part of me wanted to run, to distract myself from the onslaught of foreboding thoughts, to be home with Amelie and Ness and to escape this nightmare.

The head noise let up for a short time and our joint conviction amid many tears that night was to pray for God's complete healing or for Jesus to take him home. That night, to my surprise, we experienced the peace of God and slept. I woke up missing Josiah at 5 a.m. I wept. I prayed.

We managed to see him just before the doctors did their morning walk-around. We stroked his soft skin and perfectly formed little hands and feet and told him how much we loved him, how proud we were of him and how glad we were that he had come into our lives. We were determined to engage with him emotionally as much as possible in the time we had; he was our son and always would be.

At 9.15 a.m. I received a message from Ann Clifford – she and Steve were downstairs in the hospital. I sobbed when I received the answerphone message, greatly moved by the thoughtfulness and care of faithful friends who had cancelled their day under the nudge of the Holy Spirit. Their gentle support was just what we needed.

Agonizing uncertainty

'The future was so uncertain, with a thousand questions, but in the present I had a son and I wanted to savour every single second.'

Being able to pray, weep and talk with Ann and Steve kept us focused on the moment and praying prayers of trust to God. The future was so uncertain, with a thousand questions, but in the present I had a son and I wanted to savour every single second.

The consultant came to see us, and in the midst of our uncertainty we appreciated his directness and compassion. Josiah's condition was getting slightly worse and his heart condition wasn't fixable. We knew we had to prepare ourselves to say goodbye to our precious boy.

We went to see Josiah again shortly after 11 a.m., caressed him, prayed for him and spoke more loving words over him. Ann had brought her camera and with our permission snapped away throughout the day – these would be precious memories whatever happened.

I phoned my mum and Ness's dad to let them know we were preparing to say goodbye. My mum shared a verse that God had given her that morning from Matthew 19.14: 'Jesus said, "Let the little children come to me, and do not hinder them, for the kingdom of heaven belongs to such as these."' A gentle confirmation from a godly grandparent, who would feel this loss more than I would ever understand, that we needed to allow Josiah to go to Jesus, and who could stop him?

Preparing to say goodbye

A second visit from the consultant confirmed that Josiah was not going to live. Ness and I had already discussed that we didn't want to artificially prolong his life. From that moment on I wanted to spend every minute with him. I had a longing to be with him, and even to leave and go to the downstairs ward with Ness to get some painkillers felt like a tremendous wrench.

Every second was a valuable moment of connection. Ness and I were asked if we would like to take some handprints and footprints as Josiah lay quietly in his Perspex box. I wouldn't be changing his nappy, teaching him games, enjoying a father–son relationship. All my longing and desire to father him was being condensed into a few minutes. Condensed pain and condensed joy. I so enjoyed tending to him and wiping every last bit of ink off his little foot – it was a precious moment. I am so glad I did it.

When the final decision was made by Ness and me for Josiah to be taken out of intensive care, I felt impatient. I wanted to cuddle him. I didn't want him to die in a plastic box but peacefully in our arms. I didn't want to prolong his suffering any longer, as in death he would find his healing. I felt a quiet confidence in submitting to the God who holds the keys to life and death, and to my surprise I felt no desire to fight this decision. There was a grace to let go, to allow my poorly son to die and to be healed and made whole by our heavenly Father.

When the time came to finally hold Josiah, we were taken to a room that was tastefully decorated just along from the intensive care unit. There we waited for Josiah to be freed from all the tubes and wires. He was passed to us and we held him together. Never have we held such a precious gift, knowing that at the end of that afternoon we would never hold our baby son alive again. For the first few minutes his breathing was helped with a handheld respirator and we prayed over him and dedicated Josiah to God. These felt like the most costly prayers of my life, but at the same time felt like a tremendous privilege to pray. As I looked at Josiah my emotions were a mix of huge sadness and enormous pride – I loved this little boy and always would. After a little while all artificial breathing stimulation was taken away, and his shallow breaths continued for about ten minutes.

He died peacefully in our arms, and I believe in that same moment he became fully alive. We felt desperately sad, but not afraid, and in his death there was no fear. Beyond my own confused emotions there was a very real peace and a quiet confidence that Josiah was okay. I spontaneously prayed the Lord's Prayer and wept. This prayer had new depth, meaning and power.

'He died peacefully in our arms, and I believe in that same moment he became fully alive.'

We continued to hold, kiss and caress Josiah's little body for the next hour and outworked the counsel we had been given not to rush this time. We then took time to bathe Josiah's little body and wash his dark, curly hair. It was like a therapeutic anointing for burial, knowing that the next time we would see this little seed in a light-blue sleep suit, it would be in his new body that God has promised. Unbeknown to me, in a surprise encounter, I would see him again and get a glimpse of this future.

That evening we came back to an emotional household, where family members wept together. They were feeling our pain and the loss of a grandchild and a nephew. We sat, talked and wept that evening, and as the day drew to a close I remember the tremendous privilege I was feeling. Strange under the circumstances, but very real. I'd touched something deep in God, the veil between this life and the next had become very thin and I felt incredibly grateful to God for who he is and who he was to me, Ness, Amelie and Josiah at a time of great emotional and spiritual need. I was experiencing a peace, hope and courage that was not my own. Psalm 34.18 (NLT) declares, 'The LORD is close to the broken hearted; he rescues those whose spirits are crushed.' I was experiencing God being close in the midst of my brokenness.

Unanswered questions

Those 24 hours would shape and transform and disciple me more than any other period in my life. They formed hidden parts of my calling in ways that I struggle to articulate, although I am going to try. The tough things in your life are more connected to your calling than you may realize, and the big question is, 'What are you going to do with your pain now and in the future?'

I don't have any answers for what happened. That doesn't mean I don't have big questions. I do – lots. Having the answers to why was not going to bring Josiah back or solve the problem of my pain. I did discover that in trying to take my pain to God there were deeper comforts in his presence than any answer I might be able to articulate.

> 'How we respond to God in these times
> strengthens or weakens our sense of calling
> and determines and shapes our destiny.
> Heaven has a different perspective on our
> trials and tribulations, and by God's grace we
> can glimpse it and embrace it.'

So it was that, in the midst of family life, when Ness and I were getting on with the calling that God had given us, suffering came knocking on our door. Suffering looks different for every person and it is impossible to put ourselves in another's shoes and very difficult to imagine another's suffering. What is true in life is that suffering comes to us all in many different forms. Some is hidden away, private battles that cause great distress; other elements are broadcast for others to see, judge, gossip about, have mercy for or ignore. How we respond to our suffering is our responsibility, regardless of whether it was self-inflicted, caused by others or was simply a result of the unfairness of life. How we respond to God in these times strengthens or weakens our sense of calling and determines and shapes our destiny. Heaven has a different perspective on our trials and tribulations, and by God's grace we can glimpse it and embrace it.

All suffering causes grief. A loss of a loved one; a loss of a dream, a job, an identity, a friendship; a loss of control of some kind. The only way to move through suffering is to grieve, and it is fair to say that most of us aren't very good at grieving. We are good at feeling sorry for ourselves, but that isn't grieving. Often our pain is suppressed or compartmentalized, but the problem with unprocessed pain is that it leaks. It comes out in ways that we wouldn't choose and we struggle to control – a snappy reply, harsh words, anger, addictions, self-harm or violence. These are signs that we need God's healing and that we need space for reflection, prayer and the help of others to pinpoint the wounds from which these reactions come. A space where, if we listen beneath the noise of the pain, we can hear God tenderly asking, 'Where are you?' God is right there with us.

The gift of grief

Grief is the gift that God gives us to deal with our pain, but most of us don't access it fully because it feels scary and excruciatingly painful. We are almost afraid of the extra pain we will feel if we give ourselves to the grief journey. 'No one ever told me that grief felt so much like fear,' is how C. S. Lewis launches into his famous book on the subject.[1] However, the grief journey, when embraced, transforms us. It requires incredible courage and bravery to go on it fully; it is about surrender. It feels like dying. It is always in winter and never in summer. For Ness and me it was like a marathon and, owing to the exhaustion and the emotional distress, we were tempted to cut it short. We started very much together on this shared grief journey, but six months later, still in a world of pain, on the same beach in North Wales we were in different places. I felt numb to calling and numb to Ness. It was hard. We felt robbed of a son; we didn't want to be robbed of each other.

Engaging with grief is always really hard. It can feel like walking through thick fog, and no matter what the occasion, the cheek bones can ache and a heavy sadness sits just behind the eyes. I knew that what I didn't express, I would internalize and carry around like a dead weight. I wanted to embrace the grief as much as I could, no matter how painful. So I read books on other people's journeys of grief and loss; I journalled what I had been through and continued to experience; I even wrote a letter to Josiah, expressing my pride in him and all that I would miss being able to do with him.

I heard of a lady who was quite well-to-do who would spit, not in public, but privately, as a way of releasing some of the anger and pain. Some pain needs a physical release and a punchbag. I found myself swearing out loud, vocalizing the pain – almost always in prayer. I needed to express in language some of the torment and rage. Doing that with God who loves, accepts and understands me felt like a safe place.

We look back now on the teaching series Ness had initiated in Open Heaven before Josiah died, on the book of 1 Peter and the theme of suffering in the autumn, as divine preparation. We have a high view of Scripture that has shaped our lives and provided a foundation for trying to live life well and pursue the call of God in our glorious and messy world. Scriptures that we read in one season, and even struggled to understand at the time, came alive with revelation and hope in another. What we couldn't possibly anticipate, by the grace of God we were somehow prepared for, although we never felt prepared. This scripture in Romans is one that I have wrestled with and reflected on lots over the last decade:

> Not only that, but we rejoice in our sufferings, knowing that suffering produces endurance, and endurance produces character, and character produces hope, and hope does not put us to shame, because God's love has been poured into our hearts through the Holy Spirit who has been given to us.
>
> (Romans 5.3–5, ESV)

Suffering reframed

Rejoicing in suffering! This really doesn't make much sense from a human perspective and sounds like an oxymoron. However, the context isn't from a human perspective; it is from a God perspective, in whom and in whose sight we have been made right by faith. Out of the abundance of life in Christ we encounter the scarcity of suffering in which we must participate. Suffering in this passage is such a difficult word; failure would be much more palatable, but suffering it is.

I needed to find out more about where this word derived from in this scripture and discovered that it means to press (as in pressing grapes) or to press hard upon and to cause pressure. Pressure in our lives is something we are familiar with, and not always something we associate with suffering. It is further described as a compressed or restricted way and comes from the root Greek word *tribos*, which means a worn way or path.

This was a moment of revelation for me. I felt God reveal to me that suffering is intrinsic to life on earth; that every person who has ever lived has had to travel down the worn way of suffering. This is the human pilgrimage: to live is also to suffer. It's unavoidable; when suffering knocks at your door and you say there is no seat for him, he tells you not to worry because he has brought his own stool.[2] Indeed, as Christians we follow the suffering King who promises life to the full if we enter into his fullness of life.

So why the rejoicing? Why not just put up with the suffering? It is because the place of suffering is also the place of encounter; it is the place where we get to the end of ourselves and discover that God who knows and understands our suffering is waiting for us.

Hidden treasure

The path of suffering is also a road to discovery, and as we dare to journey with God down that road, the more we will discover about him and about ourselves. On this difficult and narrow path, treasure can be found, revelation can be found, God can be found. The prophet Isaiah reveals that in the dark nights and hard places precious gems can be found:

> And I will give you treasures hidden in the darkness –
> secret riches.
> I will do this so you may know that I am the LORD,
> the God of Israel, the one who calls you by name.
> (Isaiah 45.3, NLT)

I don't want to be prescriptive about what those hidden treasures and secret riches will be for you, but I will say that they can't be discovered in any other place. Our suffering serves to strip us back and to loosen our grip on things we weren't even aware we were grasping on to. In that place we can choose to grab hold of other things to numb the pain and relieve our discomfort, or we can choose to surrender more to the love and grace of God. Our pain can be acute in either choice; however, it is the presence of God that transforms us and our pain with repeated surrender.

> 'Our suffering serves to strip us back and to
> loosen our grip on things we weren't even
> aware we were grasping on to.'

If we don't submit our pain, we will transmit it. Submission is part of the grieving and letting go; eventually the wound becomes less tender and begins to heal. We bear a scar which in time becomes a story of God's grace that can comfort and strengthen others. Our pain, when transformed, becomes a gift to give away. Can you begin to see a link between your pain and disappointments and parts of your calling?

As we embrace our pain, we also become less fearful of other people's pain and suffering; in some cases I feel almost compelled and drawn to it. Not in a voyeuristic way, but because I know that is where God is. He really is close to the broken-hearted, and maybe I can help open a door to more of his comfort in that situation.

However, transmitted pain comes from repeatedly posturing oneself as a victim, someone who for whatever reason can't let go, can't forgive, can't face the pain, and so when the pain leaks it is by nature destructive. Hurt people hurt people. This is often unintentional, but their words and actions are informed by the burden of pain and raw nerves from an unhealed wound. If this is you, even to a very small degree, life is too short to spend half of it carrying this stuff around. It will be a blockage to your calling and lead to an unfulfilled life. Alongside the gift of grief are the gifts of forgiveness and repentance that lead us all into greater freedom and joy.

Walking together

We are all broken, and we must learn to grieve more fully and give each other permission to do so openly. Grief is the most painful gift to accept, and sometimes we need the help and encouragement of others to access it. However, generally we aren't very good at walking alongside those who grieve. Rejoicing with those who rejoice is easier; mourning with those who mourn can feel uncomfortable. Fear needs to be faced on both sides.

In every community of people there are things to celebrate wildly and things to mourn deeply going on at the same time. The church needs to be a place where both can coexist. In Acts 12 this situation is played out in an extreme way. James, the brother of John, has been killed by a sword, and it looks as though Peter will be next. Peter is going to go on trial the following day, when an angel orchestrates a miraculous escape from prison. The family and friends of James are devastated and mourning his death and the family and friends of Peter are celebrating miracles and answered prayer, all in the same church community. Why was one killed and the other spared? We don't know. We do know that heaven has a different perspective, and God's presence can be more reassuring than even the most compelling answers.

> 'In every community of people there are things
> to celebrate wildly and things to mourn deeply
> going on at the same time.'

For those grieving, we discover lots of hidden thresholds that previously we didn't know existed. The temptation is to settle for a smaller life because the associated memories can feel distressing. I spoke with a lady who had lost her husband and many years later couldn't face going back to the hospital in which he had died. This is understandable, and it also reveals that the grief journey has been cut short. Ness and I were determined that there wouldn't be any no-go areas and there wouldn't be any besetting fears associated with a place or person (little did we know we would be back at the same hospital more than 90 times in the coming years). This wasn't to be heroic; it was about our freedom and the freedom that Jesus bought for us. Even being with friends in our first church gathering after Josiah died felt vulnerable and threatening, but it was a threshold we knew we must cross early on.

For those walking alongside, it can be very intimidating, especially for those who struggle to relate to the situation that caused the grief. Open Heaven as a church was still young and this was the first death, and so we had to do a bit of coaching around what people say and do. We sent out an email to let people know what had happened and that we were happy to talk about it. That allowed people to acknowledge the loss and to express their sorrow and sadness to us. It was true in the weeks straight after that we didn't know what we wanted, so when we were asked, 'Is there anything we can do?', there wasn't. What blew us away was that people were just getting on and helping us. People thought about our practical needs: one person came round and cleaned our house from top to bottom, another took Amelie to the park many times to give us space, countless others turned up with meals and numerous gifts, and kind words were written in cards. People's love languages were in full flow as they were mourning with those who mourn.

Transformed by fire

Embracing this grief journey taught me how to submit my pain to God. Josiah's name means 'fire of God', and he was certainly that to me. His 24 hours changed my life, and my relationship with him was a furnace of transformation. Adversity that I didn't choose came my way, and while I would dearly love to have seen Josiah grow up, I would also be loath to give up the treasures I found in God through that long, dark night.

The deep sadness of grief is a dangerous place to make life decisions. What happens to calling when every ounce of enthusiasm and passion has been drained out of us? Unexpected and at times tragic life events cause us to re-evaluate and often to react. They expose or can cause weaknesses and cracks in our relationships, and these things need time. Six months into my grief journey on the beach in North Wales was one of the hardest times for me. There was a deadness and dullness in my emotions. I felt disconnected from Ness, which was scary because I love her so much, and I felt indifferent towards my work with Fusion. Life was hard and work was hard. With the help of friends, I realized that my feelings had changed but my commitments remained the same. This was not a time to react and try to kick-start positive emotions but to act out my commitments to the best of my ability. I needed to invest in my marriage and keep my calling in God simple.

The decisions we make in times and seasons of suffering are really important. They are the seeds that are planted in winter and will emerge in spring and bear fruit in summer. What fruit they bear depends on what has been sown. Will we choose to worship God with a broken heart and tears streaming down our face? Will we courageously surrender our pain and fears? Will we dare to trust that God's healing is greater than our brokenness? There is a reckless trust that comes from standing in the furnace of transformation that declares with Shadrach, Meshach and Abednego that 'the God we serve is able to deliver us from it, and he will deliver us, but even if he doesn't we aren't going to worship anyone else!' (see Daniel 3.17–18). We don't worship because we feel like it; worship is an act we choose that develops feelings for God.[3]

It is the hard times that form us and adversity that shapes us. I am learning to love and accept some of the harder places in my life. I don't travel to them alone; I invite friends on the journey and I invite God into the detail, and as I do so they become less abrasive, less threatening. We don't embrace hard times because of some masochistic tendency; we embrace them because we have to deal with them, learn from them and be transformed through them. This is our lifelong discipleship journey.

'We can be certain that God will give us the strength and resources we need to live through any situation in life that he ordains. The will of God will never take us where the grace of God cannot sustain us.'

BILLY GRAHAM

5

Calling and money: hustling with faith

Boarding the plane to San Francisco, Roger Ellis and I felt optimistic and excited. This wasn't because we were bound for the star-studded state of California – though we would later find ourselves walking a red carpet in LA – but because we felt a few transatlantic hours away from solving a rather large financial problem. Fusion needed money. Though the Bible has much to say about our lifelong relationship with money – how to steward it, not love it – it will always play a role in our lives as we seek to carry out our calling.

Fusion's finances were in a challenging place. The budget year had barely started, and in addition to the deficit against it we were carrying debt to individuals amounting to tens of thousands of pounds. Thankfully, we were now headed for a meeting with a couple of Jesus-following Silicon Valley tech billionaires. Surely, their pocket change could not only get us out of a hole but also seed the launch of Fusion in the USA?

Four years earlier, we had connected with one of the most faithful student leaders I have ever met, Dave Short, who poured himself into training Fusion small-group leaders around the USA and Mexico. Dave would be joining us in San Francisco to pitch for Fusion finance for the USA.

We settled into our accommodation, but before we had finished breakfast, our plans changed. The wealthy men we were hoping to meet that day had backed a film that was pre-miering in Hollywood that evening and said that if we were able to get ourselves to LA, we were welcome to join them. And we did, the following day returning for the very reason we came: a meeting with the people God had chosen as the solution to our problems. Or so we thought . . .

A God who provides

When we boarded that plane to San Francisco, I was full of expectation that God would provide. After all, he'd done it before. It was while I was living in my first house as a grad-uate – the 'church house' where Open Heaven had started – that I had seen answers to prayers for provision and had been surprised by the generosity of God. The large com-munal lounge, the thoroughfare from the house's hallway to the kitchen, had served as a place where time and again we had prayed and God had shown up. It boasted mercifully a brown carpet, and it was on this carpet that for nearly a month a large pile of pennies collected dust and were occa-sionally sent cartwheeling across the room from an absent-minded housemate trudging through. These pennies weren't just a result of a lack of tidying – they were a symbol of our prayers.

The others and I in the house were deeply committed to making community life flourish and seeing the church grow. The only problem was that we were all skint. I was trying to pay my fees for a year of training in evangelism, the others were hustling their way through studying with part-time work, and the bills were coming through the door, all designed to capture our attention with plenty of red ink.

Autumn arrived, the nights were drawing in and our finances had a gloomy outlook. We were fed up and a little fearful of not making ends meet. It was time to do something – we needed to break this cycle of never having 'enough'. We reasoned that if God had called us to this work, he would provide. Desperate and faith-filled, we prayed, 'Jesus, we know you love us and care about the details of our lives. Please would you make a way through this situation.'

'We reasoned that if God had called us to this work, he would provide.'

We collected the significant bundle of bills, both household and personal, and piled them together in the middle of the floor. We made declarations over our finances and prayed prayers for breakthrough. As the noise and the prayers subsided, we theatrically poured this jar of not enough pennies all over the bills, around a thousand pennies cascading down like a slot machine that had hit the jackpot. It was a symbolic, prophetic, hope-fuelled act.

We left the pennies and bills in the middle of the floor for a few weeks and resolved to get on with all that God had called us to. That's when a number of remarkable things started to happen. The first breakthrough came when we made a call to the landlord and shared that we were really struggling to pay the rent. With a generosity unheard of among landlords in student cities, he astoundingly agreed to lower our rent by £300 a month! The same week, we received a phone call from a local church in another part of the country, sharing that the church felt God had asked them to help us and offering to pay for a few months' rent to cover the cost of the venue we used for Sunday gatherings. Later that week, we received a phone call from our uni friend Graham to say that he felt God had asked him to give his car to us. He proposed to drive up, leave the keys on the kitchen table and take the train home. Favour and answers from people who knew nothing of the pennies and the prayers.

These three stories came as a quick-fire reminder that God, Jehovah Jireh, will live up to his name. Scripture reminds us time and time again that God provides. So why the conundrum? Why the doubt? Why the fear of not having enough? Alongside calling is often a sense of lack. We can't do it on our own; we haven't the talent, skills, resources or people. If you feel like this right now, you are probably on the right track. This is God's design for us, that we partner with him in his mission and with other people. We also get to lean into and learn from each other; it was never God's intention that we would be independent and self-sufficient. Rather, we take the gifts, talents, money and resources God has given us and generously give them away, generosity begetting generosity. (Ness and I would later be given four more cars and were able to give three of them away.)

> 'Alongside calling is often a sense of lack. We
> can't do it on our own; we haven't the talent,
> skills, resources or people.'

Do it again

Throughout the coming years, God's goodness and provision would surprise us again and again. Early on in our married life, Ness and I found ourselves praying for a large house so that we could live in community. It seemed impossible. We crafted a written prayer to enable us to pour out our hearts to God regardless of how faith-filled we felt. It was bold and specific, detailing the numbers and types of rooms and the purpose of the house. We had seen miraculous provision in the 'church house' and now we were praying for more miraculous provision. In my head this would mean a surprise financial gift, but I was making a huge mistake in second-guessing how God would answer this prayer.

After around six months of praying, the desire for breakthrough began to form a greater tension in me. I was struggling with a feeling of longing inside me and seeing little progress. If you feel like this, keep submitting it to God and don't give up. It isn't just about the outcome; our faith and understanding mature and grow through the process.

I took the afternoon off to share my longings and frustrations with God. After walking on my own, shouting through the woodlands outside Loughborough (what would the dog walkers think?!), I felt God gently encourage me to start looking at houses properly.

This simple encouragement set a chain of events in motion. We bought a local newspaper on the Thursday (this was before online listings were a thing!) and promptly arranged two viewings on the Friday. As soon as we crossed the threshold of the first house, we knew it wasn't right. But the second house had the opposite effect: this was the one – apart from the fact that we were £50,000 short of what we needed to buy it. I felt God say that I didn't need to do anything to bridge that gap, but on the Saturday I felt impatient, and I phoned friends and mortgage brokers to see what was possible ahead of our second viewing the following day. My own efforts and my lack of faith, contrary to what God had said, only served to leave me feeling fretful and disheartened.

That same evening, there was a knock at the door. A friend had found out that we were looking at houses and shared that she was looking to invest £50,000 somewhere. It was the confidence boost we needed to put in an offer, but we never took her money, partly because my sums were out and the real deficit was closer to £100,000! We did, however, move into the house ten weeks later. The 'miracle' involved community living and a prayerful process of discernment, testing motives and risk taking. The creative solution saw Ness, me and four friends live in this new community house, sharing food, bills and life together. This was a reminder once again that where we live and who we live with are often central to parts of God's calling on our lives as we join his mission.

> *'Money is a resource to bless and enable our calling, and God wants us to have a healthy relationship with it.'*

In praying for provision there are no formulas. It is faith that must be invested, not the same process or expected outcome. It often requires some action on our part. God knows our needs and he also wants us to work with him in working out solutions. It might start with a prophetic act or a crafted prayer; it will probably feel uncomfortable and risky at times and require perseverance. In God's economy it will lead to deeper communion with God and others and be a transformative journey. Our past experience with money means that God often has to rewire our relationship with it, and even the mention of money can be something we feel ourselves reacting to. If this is you, now is a good time to ask God what lies and fears you have around money. Money is a resource to bless and enable our calling, and God wants us to have a healthy relationship with it.

Looking back and remembering how our prayers for provision have been answered in the past helps us take steps of faith in the present and future. Fusion had seen God provide before, and so as Roger, Dave and I entered our meeting with the tech billionaires in San Francisco, we had every reason to hope God would do it again. And yet, the meeting that transpired was beyond anticlimactic. The people we met gave us their time and advice, but we didn't fit their funding criteria, for either Fusion UK or Fusion USA.

And so we returned to the UK with a slightly larger debt, thanks to two transatlantic air tickets, more red bills and a big financial challenge. A lump sum of money would have solved lots of problems, but quick fixes rarely provide lasting life lessons, and the trip reminded me again that we cannot run ahead of God's calling and expect his provision. I should have known better that in the case of a quick fix versus a faith journey, faith always wins. I don't know about you, but I find that when it comes to calling, provision and money, I have to learn the same lessons over and over again.

Scarcity scares us

Regardless of how many times we have read or experienced that God is good and desires to give good gifts to his children (see Matthew 7.11), we still tend to have a natural inclination towards scarcity over abundance. We fear not having enough, and to that end often overcompensate, on both individual and national levels. Our actions as rabid consumers act as a self-fulfilling prophecy in that when we treat goods, food and housing as scarce, they become scarce and the gap between the haves and have-nots widens.

Scarcity affects many areas of our lives. Generosity isn't just restricted to our giving of money; it also has an impact on our time, our thoughts and our conversations. To look on someone generously costs us nothing; to encourage, to praise, to compliment, to build up, to affirm or to validate – none of these things are in short supply. So why at times do I insist on making scarce what God has made abundant?

'What would it look like to choose abundance over scarcity? How would that affect your life and your calling? Life to the full in God has an abundance of love, joy, peace, patience, kindness, goodness, faithfulness, gentleness and self-control (Galatians 5.22, NLT), so why do they seem so scarce? Money is finite, but these attributes know no limits.'

Augustine writes, 'God is always trying to give good things to us, but our hands are too full to receive them.'[1] Deep down, our scarcity is about being scared. We fear that if we let go and give out then nothing will fill the void. Behind every fear is a lie. The lie that is rife in media and advertising and which has also penetrated our hearts is that there isn't enough to go around, and our identity is in what we have rather than what we have given away, in our differences rather than our commonality. What would it look like to choose abundance over scarcity? How would that affect your life and your calling? Life to the full in God has an abundance of love, joy, peace, patience, kindness, goodness, faithfulness, gentleness and self-control (Galatians 5.22, NLT), so why do they seem so scarce? Money is finite, but these attributes know no limits.

Parker Palmer writes:

True abundance comes not to those intent on securing wealth, but to those who are willing to share a life of apparent scarcity. Those who seek well-being, who grasp for more than their share, will find life pinched and fearful. They will reap only the anxiety of needing more, and the fear someday it will all be taken away. But those who live in ways that allow others to live as well, those who reach out in service to their brothers and sisters with confidence that God will meet their needs, they will find a life of plenty which transcends the economics of scarcity.[2]

It seems that however much we have, there is always a longing in us for more. But the 'more' is to be found in God. He always has more for us, and in his wisdom he will prioritize satisfying our deepest needs over nurturing our false comforts. Our satisfaction and our joy come not from having enough but from pursuing the call of the one who satisfies.

David writes of his thirst for God in Psalm 63.1:

You, God, are my God,
earnestly I seek you;

I thirst for you,
my whole being longs for you,
in a dry and parched land
where there is no water.

The characteristics of thirst are unpleasant: a dry mouth, dry skin, tiredness and headaches. We seek to avoid it, but David shows us in this psalm that thirst itself isn't bad if it is directed towards the right thing. Our thirst for money, sex and power is always lurking close by, ready to distract and divert us from the call of God, but David directs his longings towards God:

Let them give thanks to the LORD for his unfailing love
and his wonderful deeds for mankind,
for he satisfies the thirsty
and fills the hungry with good things.
(Psalm 107.8–9)

Without God we have enough to exist but not enough to be satisfied and really live. Faith in God's provision and steps of faith go together. Martin Luther King Jr is said to have described faith as taking the first step even when you don't see the whole staircase.[3] Sometimes this turns out to be a huge blessing, as the staircase can be much longer, steeper and more challenging than we would have envisaged.

A salary holiday

The trip to the USA coincided with the final weeks of transition of the leadership of Fusion from Roger to me. My calling to Fusion and this work with students was alive and well, but I was beginning to feel the mountain of financial challenges weigh heavily on my shoulders, requiring some God-given courage and creativity to continue to climb. Our failed fundraising trip looked more like an expensive holiday and paved the way for an altogether different kind of break. Big gifts for Fusion weren't forthcoming, and I knew we had to dig deep to get ourselves out of this financial hole. I was pretty sure that the solution I had been praying over – my first crucial decision as the leader of Fusion – was about to reduce our team to one. It was time to pitch the idea of a 'salary holiday' to Luke, James and Hannah on the Fusion team.

Drastic action was needed. I was tired of our team being paid late: it didn't fit with honouring the hard work they were doing, and as a movement we needed to see greater health in our relationship with finances. Externally the idea was scoffed at, but internally it felt like obedience, following a call less ordinary into a place of faith in God's provision. Together, we were all going on a 'salary holiday' for three months. It wasn't the sort of holiday we were used to, or would have chosen, but it was another opportunity to trust in God and to outwork calling despite our obvious lack. Support and encouragement soon came from friends and churches, and a conviction for the importance of the work deepened. The Fusion team would continue working, knowing they weren't going to be paid, but would be provided for through the generosity of friends and strangers.

When these tests and challenges come along, we have to dare to take God at his word, trusting that in seeking first his kingdom all these things will be added to us (see Matthew 6.33).

Three months later, the finances were in order and no one has been paid late since. We were also unwittingly sowing the seeds for another financial breakthrough years later.

Faith can feel and seem reckless at times and can cause raised eyebrows from those looking in. Well-meaning friends who aren't undergoing the same training programme God has you on will question how sensible and sustainable it is. This all serves to push us into prayer and to find peace in our convictions. I want to ask you, are there reckless things you need to do when it comes to pursuing your calling? Things that aren't sensible and could leave you feeling misunderstood? We don't go hunting for these challenges, but sometimes to break through the invisible barriers we need to do something less ordinary.

I and the Fusion team have a dream that every student will find hope in Jesus and a home in a local church. From a human perspective it is neither sensible nor realistic, yet because of the one who called us we are prepared to go to some extreme lengths to see it happen.

What dreams do you carry? What are the desires and longings that never really go away? How far will you go to see them come about? No dream becomes a reality without sacrifice. Often the lessons we learn are so much more valuable than money. Don't let money be a barrier to you stepping into your calling.

Fundraising

When I dream about the student mission field in Europe that consists of 25 million students, I can't help but pray for more workers. My work with Fusion has brought me into contact with many fascinating and faithful people: I have been able to hang out with the Navigators in the Netherlands and Every Nation leaders in Berlin. Their student ministries have been able to release dozens of workers by equipping individuals to raise their own finance through an approach called Partner Support. Partner Support doesn't ask for sponsors, donors or investors. Instead, it invites people to partner in the work and ministry through giving, prayer, communication and friendship.

I saw how inviting financial partners is part of God's design. It had blessed the work of other student ministries and I had a growing sense it would do the same for Fusion. After all, this approach was instrumental in Jesus' ministry (Luke 8.1–3), and was essential for countless pioneers in church history and even in the translation of the Bible into English. The seeds that were sown with reckless faith during our 'salary holiday' were now germinating.

> *'When we are called by God to work for him,*
> *he will provide what we need to outwork that*
> *calling. Do you believe that?'*

Reading Henri Nouwen's book, *A Spirituality of Fundraising*, I felt faith, expectancy and even excitement about this Partner Support approach begin to rise. When we are called by God to work for him, he will provide what we need to outwork that calling. Do you believe that? It is also true that God's provision frequently comes through people, often those in his Church. Nouwen writes:

Asking people for money is giving them the opportunity of putting their resources at the disposal of the

Kingdom, it is giving other people the chance of offering their resources for the work of God. Secondly, asking people for money is inviting them into a new communion (the things we share and hold in common). This is very important; asking for money is inviting people into your vision. 'We want you to get to know us. We want you to enter into communion with us.'[4]

This challenge came around the time I was turning 40. Perhaps that's a long way off for many of you. And yet, milestones often throw up a lot of fears about where we 'should' be in life. Our daughter Amelie now had a little sister called Lauren, Ness and I had a mortgage – and I was going to be 40! Surely, I shouldn't be asking people to raise my salary? And yet, through Nouwen's book God revealed how so often our reluctance to ask for money is rooted in pride, self-sufficiency and the fear of being rejected. I battled all three!

I wonder how you feel about money. How do you feel about asking for money? How do you feel about being asked to share your money? How do you feel about the words of Jesus when he says, 'It is more blessed to give than to receive' (Acts 20.35)? One of the first steps I took was to partner more intentionally with a number of people financially and invest in them and their calling.

Nouwen concludes by saying:

Fundraising then is a very rich and beautiful activity. It is an integral part of our ministry. In fundraising we discover that we are all poor and that we are all rich, and in ministering to each other – each from the riches that he or she possesses – we work together to build the Kingdom of God.

I chatted to Ness and to many others and even met a handful of people who said they only ever asked God for money; they wouldn't ask people. I admired their position but disagreed theologically: we need each other, and we need to be free to share our needs with each other. Challenges around finance, relationships, health, family and work are to be shared. Partnership in the kingdom is always a two-way commitment and it always leads to deeper communion.

Partner Support was the way forward. I was sold on how it fitted with God's economy for building deeper relationships and commitments and financed God's mission to students. While it involved some risks, took some navigating internally and some wrestling with nagging doubts, I am pleased to say that, within a few years, I and the Fusion team were all close to raising 100 per cent of our salary and expenses. Not only that, we have all been able to share our lives at a deeper level, to invite others on the journey and to create space for others to participate. These are wonderful things money can't buy and we can only receive by giving!

A Spirituality of Fundraising challenged us all deeply. Before anyone on the Fusion team starts to invite people to partner with them, their first task is to retreat with God and that book and ask God to highlight all their hang-ups with money. John Wesley is known for having said that the last part of a person to be converted is his or her wallet. When that conversion takes place, greed, pride and scarcity give way to generosity, stewardship and abundance. This move to the Partner Support model is enabling more student workers to join this mission. Dozens of people continue to pour forward, articulating a calling to student mission and being willing to raise their own finance. Practically, needs are being met and workers who deserve their wages (see Luke 10.7) are being paid. This is the same 'partnership in the gospel' (Philippians 1.5) that the apostle Paul celebrates and encourages in the lives of believers.

It is often the case with God that our apparent failures turn into valuable life lessons. In chasing an American dream we ended up more convinced of God's dream for us. The failed fundraising trip and salary holiday laid strong foundations of conviction for God's calling, and first and foremost we don't trust in money; we trust in God. In God, we are led down all kinds of creative paths and avenues so that calling can be both sharpened and outworked. Our hustle with faith is trusting that as we seek first God's kingdom, we will have all that we need to be faithful to God's calling on our lives. It is unlikely to be ordinary or conventional, but it will be accompanied by faith and peace.

For each of us, the journey with money will be different, but the principles and values will be the same. We are all called to be generous with what we have, to make sacrifices and to steward and share resources well. When we respond to what God is calling us to be and to do, we will not have what it takes or have enough. It will require hard work and facing some fears. We will be forced to put our faith in God and enter into his abundance. The fact that it is God who is hiring us will ensure we have the provision we need.

Now is the time to take steps of faith and to test the calling. Not having enough money is not a valid excuse when it comes to outworking our calling, and entering into more of God's calling will always feel risky and contested. As a family we were about to find ourselves contesting once again and fighting some new battles in the pursuit of the fullness of life God has for us; moments that would require us to stand firm even though the circumstances were about to bring us to our knees.

'To learn strong faith is to endure great trials. I have learned my faith by standing firm amid severe testings.'

GEORGE MUELLER

6

Calling and battles: I will stand

'Our Father who is in heaven . . .' The same prayer I had spontaneously prayed in the wake of Josiah's death would be often on my lips over the next season; it would help me pray when I didn't know what to pray. On this occasion, the prayer was being whispered just under my breath as I knelt behind a giant, five-foot-high Connect 4 puzzle in a hospital waiting room. My 20-month-old daughter, Lauren, was in the adjacent room having an X-ray of her chest. The room had a sterile, over-clean smell, the lighting harsh with fluorescent bright white light.

There were other people in the waiting room, but I didn't care. I was desperate, so there I was, on my knees in a small children's play area, pleading with God for mercy and healing. You might think that my journey with Josiah would have prepared me for some of the battles that lay ahead, but more often than not they appear from nowhere, and sometimes all we can do in the pursuit of our calling is to stand.

Connect 4 – the aim of the game is simply to make a row of four counters of the same colour. You and your opponent take turns to drop a counter into one of seven slots. My prayer was about connection: I needed more; I needed to make a four. I needed to know that Father, Son and Spirit were aligned with my torment and suffering, that they weren't distant and that we were connected. I needed to hear

God call me again – '*Ayeka*?' – to know that God was deeply concerned about where I was.

Ten weeks earlier Ness and I had been away as a family at a summer festival and I was changing Lauren's nappy. She was a delight: playful and smiley with big blue eyes and curly blonde locks. My gaze would be fixed on her, a magnetic pull towards her small and perfectly formed facial features. Some sort of silent affirming conversation was taking place, and I was absentmindedly massaging her chubby thighs when I felt a pea-sized knot in her hamstring.

Once home from the festival, we mentioned it to a doctor. Minimal concern was expressed and we were told that 'we all have lumps and bumps'. However, this never felt satisfactory and the 'pea' was growing, so we arranged an appointment with our local GP, who was brilliant. She immediately referred Lauren for tests at Leicester Royal Infirmary, where ultrasounds, X-rays and MRIs would all look to shed some light on a diagnosis and pinpoint what was going on. Numerous trips to the hospital had not yet revealed the cause of the lump, but that was about to change.

It was 2 November, a Monday, and it was reasonable to question why it was necessary for seven people to be squeezed into a small consultant's room. The signs were ominous. Ness and I were both seated, holding Lauren, as the doctor began to speak. Ness already had tears rolling down her cheeks before he mentioned the cancer. She knew – we both knew – but it was still a shock, a body blow, to hear the word. Our beautiful little girl had cancer, and the tumour had quickly grown to the size of a golf ball.

Within minutes we were being shown round the children's cancer ward. Was this really happening? I felt as though I was in a trance, but this was no dream; it was a real-life nightmare we hadn't chosen but which we would have to navigate.

The treatment and tests would start immediately. Over the next eight days Lauren would have four general anaesthetics, MRIs, blood and bone-marrow tests and an operation to attach a tube called a Hickman line which was connected into a main artery in her chest at one end. The other end would dangle out of her chest so blood could be taken easily and chemotherapy administered. She would also have a chest X-ray to determine whether any cancer had spread to her lungs.

A scenario with a sinister outlook. What do you do in these moments? All kinds of fears were bombarding my mind, and adrenaline was c oursing through my veins. I felt deeply afraid and perceived a grave sense of threat to the well-being of my family. No one had died, but the shadow of death loomed, affecting my vision and thoughts. It was a valley that I had been in not too long before, and it was too soon to be journeying through again.

Except I had no choice. This was another path of suffering we would have to walk. Four days after receiving the diagnosis, there I was, kneeling behind the giant Connect 4 and trembling with fear, praying, 'Our Father . . .' In that particular moment, there was no sudden shift in my emotions or fears. It was a declaration. It was how I would fight this battle. It was setting my true north in the midst of uncertainty: my inner compass was going to point to my Father.

Frederick Buechner talks about the need for boldness when praying the Lord's Prayer and says that all too often we pray it unthinkingly. 'Thy will be done' is what we are saying. That is the climax of the first half of the prayer. We are asking God to be God. We are asking God not to do what we want but to do what God wants. We are asking God to make manifest the holiness that is now mostly hidden, to set free in all its terrible splendour the devastating power that is now mostly under restraint. 'Thy kingdom come . . . on earth', is what we are saying. To speak these words is to invite the tiger out of the cage, to unleash a power that makes an atomic power look like a warm breeze.[1]

Buechner goes on to say that it really is only the words 'Our Father' that make it bearable. None of this is going through my head as I am praying it; I just know it is a powerful prayer and I am really desperate. We don't need to feel powerful or full of faith to pray powerful prayers, and thankfully God understands this better than we do. He isn't fazed by our weakness, doubts, fears or the situations we find ourselves in. He calls us close and invites us to share what we'd struggle to say to others or even to find the words to vocalize at all. Lovingly and gently he asks, 'Where are you?' And before we have time to reply he makes room at his table and beckons us to be with him.

God's kitchen table

Hanging on our kitchen wall at home we have a print of *Trinity* by the Russian painter Andrei Rublev. It was painted as an icon for the abbot of the Trinity Monastery of St Sergius in Russia when they were facing persecution around 1410. The inspiration for the painting is Genesis 18, where Abraham entertains three mysterious strangers. He greets them by bowing low to the ground and offers them rest and hospitality. The three agree to Abraham's offer in unison and the Genesis writer refers to them as 'they' or 'the Lord'.

In Rublev's painting he depicts the three heavenly visitors sitting around a table with a single cup at the centre. They are Father, Son and Spirit. The Spirit is seated on the right with head inclined towards the Father and the Son. However, the Spirit's gaze is towards the open space at the table. That's right, there is space for another. A dinner invitation to dine at God's place and to sit round his kitchen table. There is only one problem with the table – the view. You can see your enemies all around.

> Even though I walk through the valley of the shadow
> of death,
> I will fear no evil,
> for you are with me;
> your rod and your staff,
> they comfort me.
> You prepare a table before me
> in the presence of my enemies;
> you anoint my head with oil;
> my cup overflows.
> (Psalm 23.4–5, ESV)

One of the challenges about living as a Christian is that it creates more tensions to live with. We believe in a God who is defined by love and is all powerful and could alleviate our suffering in a moment. And occasionally there are moments – signs, if you will – where God responds to our prayers and a little bit of the kingdom of heaven breaks in. They are moments of miracles and healing and they are signs of a divine reality yet to be fully revealed. It happens not according to any framework of understanding we have but according to the wisdom of God.

It seems that God also lives these tensions, for what he could alleviate or solve with his power, in his wisdom he demonstrates unfathomable patience and restraint. The prophet Isaiah reminds us:

'For my thoughts are not your thoughts,
neither are your ways my ways,'
declares the LORD.
'As the heavens are higher than the earth,
so are my ways higher than your ways
and my thoughts than your thoughts.'
(Isaiah 55.8–9)

Called to communion

The comfort we crave is not going to be found in God's answers, nor in his power breaking in to change our situation. The comfort we need is realized in his presence. In whose presence shall I reside when fears and lies crowd my heart and mind? The invitation to dine with God mercifully doesn't come to us as people who have earned it by good works, by moving in the right circles or by regular devotion. It comes to all: all who hunger, all who thirst, all who recognize their need of a doctor.

> *'The comfort we crave is not going to be found in God's answers, nor in his power breaking in to change our situation. The comfort we need is realized in his presence.'*

It is in these moments that our truest and purest sense of calling is experienced. We are called to be close. We are called to communion. Close communion to all that God is and wants to be to us. It is only this closeness that means we can contend with the enemies that surround us. Our enemies are called many things, but near the top are Fear, Worry and Lies. They are all too ready to engage with us, distort and distract us from God's calling, and to do so especially when we feel weak and tired.

This all sounds good in theory, but how? How do you feast in the presence of your enemies? Where do you look? What do you focus on? I have found that weakness and worship go well together. In our vulnerability and need, choosing to focus on the goodness of God despite our circumstances is outworking who we are called to be. Worship is a spiritual battle cry and the best way to disarm fears, worries and lies. Our enemies see that we belong to Jesus. Jesus does the fighting; we do the feasting. So many of the psalms live this tension; humanity has been here many times before and the songs of pilgrimage that the psalms (120–134) record are there for us to meditate on and find comfort in.

Songs for battle

One of the practices that sustained me during what would become a gruelling nine-month journey of hospital visits, blood counts and uncertainty was worship. I was drawn to listen to an album by Godfrey Birtill called *Very God*. Many of the songs seemed to bring comfort and had a strong resonance with what Ness and I were both feeling and facing. In fact, I didn't listen to anything else. Many of the lyrics captured the prayers I hadn't yet been able to articulate. As the chemo kicked in, it wouldn't be long before the last of

Lauren's beautiful curly blonde hair would fall out. I needed an outlet for my grief, rage and anger, and the songs were full of Scripture and declarations about who God is and the hope we have in him. I'd often just turn up the volume and lie on the floor.

This wasn't a season in which I was looking to make lots of gains and progress; it was just about standing my ground. I identified with the heartfelt cries that come through the Psalms, songs and lyrics that have helped people connect with God in all kinds of circumstances for the last 3,000 years. I added my voice to the long line of saints who have declared, 'I have taken a stand, and I will publicly praise the Lord' (Psalm 26.12, NLT Open Bible). We worship God because he is good, not because our circumstances are good.

The cancer Lauren had was rare; most doctors would never come across it in their lifetime. It was a surprise, therefore, to learn that just up the road in Lincoln, church leaders Stuart and Irene Bell had recently been on a similar journey with their son, David, fighting an identical type of cancer. I phoned Stuart for any advice, prayer and wisdom he had to offer; he had lots. One of the remarkable insights that came from that conversation was a story Stuart told me about how they made their stand in the face of such terror. For a time in their journey they would gather together for prayer and worship, and in that season a number of songs were written to help them pray, worship and make declarations. The songs were written by Godfrey Birtill and were the very ones I had been drawn to listen to and couldn't stop playing!

After I've done everything, I will stand
With my eyes on my King of kings, I will stand.

I will stand: I will stand in confidence
To see the Lord's deliverance,
Yes I will stand.
I will stand: of this I'm absolutely sure,
I'll see the goodness of the Lord,
Yes I will stand.
Because I'm standing with Jesus,
I am standing with my King.
Because I'm standing with Jesus,
I am standing with my King.
Even in the darkest days, I will stand,
And bring a sacrifice of praise, I will stand.
I will stand: no matter what is thrown at me,
I'll stand against the devil's schemes,
Yes I will stand.
I will stand: upright and undisturbed,
Unafraid I'm standing firm,
Yes I will stand.
Stand, and I will stand with you.
Stand, and I will stand with you.
Stand, and I will stand with you.[2]

The timing of the battle against cancer felt incredibly sinister, and it had the sulphurous smell of an enemy scheme. The teachings of Jesus are very clear that we have an adversary who wants to rob, steal and kill, and we are to be on our guard and make our stand. After 15 years of meeting in school halls, Open Heaven was making a bid to restore a closed-down church building in the centre of town and had recently launched a fundraising campaign. At the same time, Fusion was starting a 20-venue tour around UK university cities to inspire students to share their faith with boldness and love. Both felt strategic, important acts of kingdom obedience which were being challenged and threatened through this trial. Ness and I, as well as fighting for the life of our daughter, believed that our calling was also being contested, and I had no doubt in my mind that the two were connected.

Loving the university

The thinking behind the Fusion tour had come from a prophetic and prayerful response to a headline in *The Guardian* that read 'Christian group to take university to court'.[3] Frustrated, saddened and depressed by another negative portrayal of Christianity in the media and angry that this was specific to the universities, I knew there had to be a better way. Surely we are to be good news, building bridges and relationships, eating and drinking together with those who don't share our views and values; willing to risk being tarred with the same brush of accusation that Jesus faced as he dined and hung out with those scorned and possibly sued by the religious.

I took it to God in prayer: 'Father, are we really supposed to be suing our universities? Is that how your kingdom is going to come? By lawsuits and litigation? By demanding our rights?'

I felt the answer was loud and clear: 'Don't sue the university; love the university!' God commands us to love him, to love our neighbour, to love our enemies, and so of course we are to love our universities. God is love and wants us to love the university, the students, the cleaners, the lecturers, the caterers, the whole lot. This is the message we must bring to the university cities. Christianity on campus badly needed a rebrand around its central message, and so we began to talk about love – the most talked-about, written-about, sung-about topic in the history of the world. Not just any old love, however, but God's love.

God's primary and most glorious attribute is that of love. This love is not a concept or a romantic ideal, but an eternal, enduring, sacrificial love that causes hardened hearts to melt and cynics to dance. A love that isn't an ethereal idea but is to be experienced. For people to love God they have to experience something of God's love for them. This is how we are made: we are made to love God. It is in the DNA of every human being; buried beneath the sin and the selfishness is the ability to respond to God's love and to love God back.

God's love doesn't come gift-wrapped or in the form of a consumer package. Today's advertisers would struggle to brand this love. This love is not for gaining riches or for exploiting people's weaknesses. This love is not exclusive or choosy. This love cannot target a specific people group on the basis of their income, background, apparent worth or contribution to society. This love doesn't carry a price tag to receive it, or an education to understand it. It mysteriously clings to his followers, inescapable through life's high points and darkest days. A love so strong and so committed that nothing can separate us from it.

Is this the sort of message the enemy would scheme against and look to halt? I think so. We were making our stand, and as the 'loveyouruni' tour had started just a week before Lauren's diagnosis, my participation was in jeopardy.

My war dance

As well as my quietly mumbled declaration behind the supersized Connect 4, I felt convicted to keep my commitments on a number of tour dates if they didn't clash with Lauren's treatment. This was a different sort of declaration that I felt compelled to roar; this was part of my war dance against the schemes of the enemy. A raised fist that declared, 'I'm not backing down and I refuse to be intimidated.' It wasn't very coordinated and it lacked energy at times; however, it gave some much-needed expression to active prayer and worship during those crazy early weeks of diagnosis and treatment.

On 11 November the 'loveyouruni' tour reached Leeds. We had some seminars organized for the daytime and then a gathering planned in St George's Church in the evening. The previous nine days had been a roller coaster of emotions and, all things considered, I was feeling OK about speaking that evening. That was until my phone rang around 6 p.m. It was Dr Visser from the hospital. Dr Visser was our consultant; he was tall with silvery hair and kind eyes. He was a good man, but this time he didn't bring good news. 'The tests on Lauren's bone marrow were inconclusive. We need to do the test again,' were his words.

'I'm sorry,' I said, 'what do you mean "inconclusive"?' Any tiredness in my body was now more than compensated for by my racing thoughts.

Dr Visser calmly explained, 'We couldn't rule out for certain that the cancer hasn't spread to her bones. We need to test again. I need your permission for another general anaesthetic and lumbar puncture. Please can you bring her in tomorrow?'

There would be many times I'd sink to my knees during this cancer journey; fortunately not too many where I was going to be preaching soon after. Time and again we hear that when we are weak, God is strong, and that in our weakness he uses us more powerfully. I think this is sometimes true, but the reality is that when we are weak we are tempted to quit, and God can't use us at all if we do!

I somehow picked myself up off the floor to try to cast vision for a brighter student future to the few dozen people who had gathered. I remember nothing of what I shared that evening, but there were others in the room who remember what God spoke to them. A student from York called Miriam had come over for the evening, and for her this would be where she could identify a moment of God's calling on her life, an ignition moment. The spirit and the message of the 'loveyouruni' tour was designed to be caught and embodied. Five years later, Miriam would not only find herself a key leader in the Fusion movement, but she would also champion the same message. Over a two-year period, Miriam and her less-than-reliable orange VW Camper Van would travel more than 3,000 miles, stopping to ignite churches and students in every university city in the UK.

Battling on

Ness and I battled on with the building project, we battled on with the tour and mainly we battled on with the cancer journey. It wasn't about giving the projects lots of energy – we didn't have any. It was about putting one foot in front of another when we could, and when we couldn't, learning simply to stand. Once again, the energy and passion we would normally feel for the work we believed God had called us to was missing, but while some fairly big circumstances had changed, our calling hadn't.

The seasons where we feel weak and vulnerable are rarely times to make big decisions. Our emotions are an unreliable compass for setting direction in life at the best of times. Being kind to ourselves and others and focusing on our core commitments need to be higher priorities when the pressure is on and life feels out of control. How kind have you been to yourself recently? I am not talking about giving yourself fake comforts; rather I am talking about doing things that replenish and restore you; doing things that look after you, such as opening up to a friend, making time for exercise, a retreat day, an early night.

> 'Being kind to ourselves and others and
> focusing on our core commitments need to be
> higher priorities when the pressure is on and
> life feels out of control. How kind have you
> been to yourself recently?'

Lauren was getting lots of attention and it was important that Amelie was given an equal amount. For Ness and me, it was about trying to support each other as we faced down the fears of what Lauren was enduring. It was also about trying to do some normal things that young families do, although things like swimming and being around crowds were not possible with the chemo destroying Lauren's immune system and increasing the probability of infection.

It wasn't fair. So much of what life deals us is outside our control. However, it could have been worse – a lot worse. We live in the UK in an age where healthcare is free and healing drugs have been developed. The chemo was crude – it is essentially a poison that kills the cancer and it could have killed Lauren if it wasn't for many litres of fluid flushing it out of her system and bloating her little body each round of treatment. Born in another part of the world or in another era, she would have died. Despite great advancements, a number of the children on Lauren's cancer ward are no longer with us. Life isn't fair, and because the treatment was healing Lauren we felt like grateful beneficiaries of life's unfairness. Perspective helps us persevere and to be thankful in the midst of our suffering.

Sticky labels

The nine-month battle with cancer also had an impact on my identity. In making our stand, what we stand on can be the difference between a firm foundation and shaky ground. A battle rages over our identity when we have been through challenging and traumatic life events; there is a part of us, which we could call 'the victim', that cries, 'Don't you know what I've been through?' Maybe because of life's unfairness or harshness we can feel entitled to more – a little more grace and leeway from people to somehow balance things out. Life now owes us something back. Maybe you can recognize some of these feelings in yourself.

This thinking is not especially calculated, more unprocessed, and it is our true identity that is at stake. I became aware that I was wearing labels like lanyards. One read, 'Bereaved parent'; the other, 'Child with cancer'. Hanging around my neck, they were beginning to define me and even get in the way of both my freedom and my calling. We can all be tempted to wear them, especially when wounds have been inflicted on us by others or by life's lottery: 'abused', 'bullied', 'betrayed', 'excluded', 'depressed', 'confused', 'physical pain', 'illness'. You can add your own. It is so tempting to wear the label, to elicit more encouragement and affirmation from others, which we of course need. The danger is that labels become sticky and attach themselves to our identity. We have to be very deliberate about peeling them off.

There was a subtle tipping point to the empathy and compassion of others becoming something that would stop me taking responsibility for dealing with my pain. Pain can become a distorted comfort in these situations and can even manipulate others by drawing out of them more than they want to give, to feed the open wound in our life. God wants to clean and close the wound, and only he is able to do that. Os Guinness once observed, 'It is the unrivaled wonder of the gospel of Jesus Christ that no other God has wounds.'[4] Edward Shillito (1872–1948), a Free Church minister in England during the First World War, wrote this poem:

> If we have never sought, we seek Thee now;
> Thine eyes burn through the dark, our only stars;
> We must have sight of thorn-pricks on Thy brow,
> We must have Thee, O Jesus of the Scars.
> The heavens frighten us; they are too calm;
> In all the universe we have no place.
> Our wounds are hurting us; where is the balm?
> Lord Jesus, by Thy Scars, we claim Thy grace.
> If, when the doors are shut, Thou drawest near,
> Only reveal those hands, that side of Thine;

We know to-day what wounds are, have no fear,
Show us Thy Scars, we know the countersign.
The other gods were strong; but Thou wast weak;
They rode, but Thou didst stumble to a throne;
But to our wounds only God's wounds can speak,
And not a god has wounds, but Thou alone.

What has happened in my life doesn't define me – only Christ defines me. The same can be true for you. 'But to our wounds only God's wounds can speak' – we can only derive so much comfort from others before we allow God's wounds to have the final say:

But he was pierced for our transgressions,
he was crushed for our iniquities;
the punishment that brought us peace was on him,
and by his wounds we are healed.
(Isaiah 53.5)

True identity

It is the kindness of God that leads us to repentance (see Romans 2.4), and that is what I had to do when I realized the lanyards that bore labels of false identity were distorting who God was calling me to be. Taking off the imaginary lanyards was a moment in a much bigger process of healing and was about aligning myself more fully with my Healer than my pain.

I am also convinced that this healing journey has a profound impact on our calling in Christ. What were once sharp and sensitive areas of pain become sensitive areas of empathy towards others. By the grace of God, he takes our pain and transforms it to be a blessing to others. For many of us, this divine exchange unlocks new depths of calling as we partner with God in ministering to a broken world.

Beyond our wounds, our identity isn't in our achievements, our success, our pain, our failure, our sexuality, our education or our relationship status. Eugene Peterson translates Galatians 3.28, 'In Christ's family there can be no division into Jew and non-Jew, slave and free, male and female.' We could add black and white, single and married, victim and perpetrator. None of those identities is primary and all must be surrendered because, 'Among us you are all equal. That is, we are all in a common relationship with Jesus Christ' (Galatians 3.28, MSG).

In some things we get to choose whether we persevere in them; other things choose us. The journey with Lauren to treat the cancer in her leg was one we didn't get to choose. It turned out to be an intensive and exhausting nine months, including 90 visits to the hospital, numerous overnight stays and living with a heightened sense of threat as every three weeks the chemotherapy nuked her immune system. I would be back in the Connect 4 room another dozen times, I'd pray the Lord's Prayer over and over again, and as the visits stacked up I'd do so from a place of greater peace. The many days spent on the children's cancer ward felt like being in Neverland: time seemed to stop; it was other-worldly, away from the 'real life' that we had known. The outworking of my calling to church and students felt like it was being continually disrupted, but in reality my calling was being deepened. I regularly found myself like the lost son – I had nothing to offer; I just needed the embrace of the

Father. That was enough for God, and slowly I was learning that it was enough for me too.

> *'The outworking of my calling to church and students felt like it was being continually disrupted, but in reality my calling was being deepened. I regularly found myself like the lost son – I had nothing to offer; I just needed the embrace of the Father.'*

The year was hard and felt hard; the tour was hard and felt like a failure, but seeds were being sown in the darkness, of which I had no comprehension. We were carried by others, their prayers and their kindness. From the moment of diagnosis, the church rallied. On opening the curtains during that traumatic first week, Ness saw two of our students standing like sentries on the corners of our driveway. Praying for our broken family, they had been there all night.

Their prayers and ours were answered. Lauren, to her credit, endured much, maintained her readiness to laugh and smile, and made a full recovery.

The stands we make, whether large or small, are important. They help us to live life's tensions well, in a world that is messy and glorious, in fields where wheat grows alongside weeds, where blessings overflow and battles rage, and where grace abounds in the midst of suffering. They help us push through difficulties and disappointments and they help us persevere into more of our calling and the life God has for us.

'The LORD directs the steps of the godly.

He delights in every detail of their lives.

Though they stumble, they will never fall,

for the LORD holds them by the hand.'

PSALM 37.23–24 (NLT)

7

Calling and perseverance: grace and grit

The Lord directs our steps, but that doesn't mean he will take us on what we imagine is the most direct route towards our destination. It might well be that you are taken on a route that starts in a completely different direction from where you ultimately want to go. I have long chased after the dream God has put on my heart – to see students find hope in Jesus and a home in the local church – but in following that dream I have experienced setbacks, detours and rerouting as I have tried to walk out my calling. I imagine that to a greater or lesser extent you can relate to this.

Eugene Peterson borrowed a phrase from Friedrich Nietzsche and wrote a book about it – *A Long Obedience in the Same Direction*. For the Christian, this phrase contains much to nourish us and give us perspective, not just for the moment, but for the movement in our life. The heart of calling is to respond to God's call every day. And it was about to take on greater meaning for me and a handful of the Fusion team as our desire to see thousands of churches welcoming and sharing Jesus with millions of students would lead us to establish Student Linkup.[1]

It was a big dream – setting up an initiative to help local churches to be ready to welcome students wherever they went to study in the world. It would also take a lot of people, technology, resources and finance to see it happen. The big dream called for a big sponsorship challenge, and that's why I and the Fusion team found ourselves setting off along the River Thames towpath from Marlow to Central London, a journey that would see us walk long and obediently for 50 miles non-stop in the same direction.

An easy start

It was mid-June. The walk started in warm sunshine outside a pub in Marlow. I'd travelled down with Matt and Phil, who were heading up the support team, and it wasn't long before we were greeting Luke and Miriam and other Fusion team members. The mood among the 15 walkers was buoyant: smiles, laughter, excitement and nervous energy for what lay ahead.

Starting well was easy. It didn't require any conscious effort. I didn't notice putting one foot in front of the other – a technique perfected so long ago that most of us take it for granted. Conversation, joking around, surrounded by beautiful scenery, we were completely distracted from the very act that was the main event – walking.

Walking allows us to notice things, people, animals, the changing seasons, how we are doing, our mood and emotions. This is not only true in the literal sense. When life is slowed down to walking pace it gives us opportunity to reflect and plan, to daydream and imagine, to become curious again and able to ponder the thoughts and questions the rest of life hasn't had time for. 'Unimpeded walking is one of life's most ordinary, least expensive, and deeply rewarding pleasures. With little effort, putting one foot in front of the other and going forward can provide a foretaste of heaven.'[2]

Slowing to a walk can also help us detect God's perspective on our lives and the way we are walking. Most importantly perhaps, it affords us the time to question whether we are walking in step with him. It takes time to learn how to walk with God. A life that is on course with God is one that has submitted control to the Holy Spirit. The apostle Paul declares, 'If we live by the Spirit, let us also walk in the Spirit' (Galatians 5.25, NKJV). It is the Holy Spirit who then begins to produce all kinds of wonderful fruit in our lives as we walk out our calling.

> *'Slowing to a walk can also help us detect God's perspective on our lives and the way we are walking. Most importantly perhaps, it affords us the time to question whether we are walking in step with him. It takes time to learn how to walk with God.'*

Although going in the same direction, we all walk differently and at different paces. It wouldn't be long before the 15 walkers and a few friends were fanning out, finding their rhythm, the task-focused marchers leading the way and the people-focused saunterers ambling behind.

Soon, 20 minutes had flown by and so had the first mile. Walking with friends on a warm summer's day to raise money – why hadn't we thought of this before? It was enjoyable and easy. Those early miles required only small amounts of energy and little in the way of perseverance.

However, having never walked that far in one go before, what wasn't obvious was that how we walked in the early miles would affect our later miles: our footwear, clothing, fluids, nutrition were good for ten miles, but how about for 30 or 50 miles?

Muddy paths

'Liquid history' is how the nineteenth-century MP John Burns described the River Thames. It is a delightful description that evokes memories of times gone by and how the river has brought life to villages, towns and the mighty city of London. Much more than a water source, it has transported goods, provided energy for the industrial mills and, more recently, brought cooling for power stations. The river has been a curator of history and shaped the landscape of modern London. The Thames path we were walking stretches for 160 miles, and we were following in the footsteps of many who had laid foundations for the amenities we enjoy today.

Like the river, our walk with God has a history that stretches back to a garden. In the midst of our digital age there is an ancient path to be walked, and yet, as the prophet Jeremiah lamented, we can so easily find ourselves on muddy paths:

> But my people are not so reliable, for they have deserted
>   me;
> they burn incense to worthless idols.
> They have stumbled off the ancient highways
> and walk in muddy paths.
> (Jeremiah 18.15, NLT)

Who and what we look to when we are walking will determine our direction. Our eyes and attention can so easily be drawn to false gods and worthless idols; in pursuit of money and fame is the way much of the world walks. On closer inspection, we see that people's lives have been muddied with greed, envy, insecurity and selfishness. Beneath the shine of idols is the grime of unhappy lives still searching for purpose, meaning and calling.

> 'Who and what we look to when we are
> walking will determine our direction.'

So how do we walk in such a way that leads to contentment, joy and peace in our lives? 'You're blessed when you stay on course, walking steadily on the road revealed by God,' the psalmist in Psalm 119.1–2 (MSG) says. 'You're blessed when you follow his directions, doing your best to find him.'

Obedience has a history

It might feel as if you're alone, like a pilgrim on a road. No one is in front of you, beside you or behind you. Yet you are not alone; multitudes have trodden the pilgrim paths before you. Generation after generation has chosen to walk the God way, to respond to his call, and now it is our turn. The way may look overgrown in today's culture, with new technology and information crowding in on the path, but the prayers of the saints still leave their mark. The signs are there when we slow down to walking pace – prayers that linger in the air and have littered the landscape of Europe with stone chapels and churches. God has been here before, he is with us now, and the future belongs to him.

Eugene Peterson writes, 'Christians tramp well-worn paths: obedience has a history.' He goes on to say:

This history is important, for without it we are at the mercy of whims. Memory is the databank we use to evaluate our position and make decisions. With biblical memory we have two thousand years of experience from which to make off-the-cuff responses that are required each day in the life of faith. If we are going to live adequately and maturely as the people of God, we need more data to work from than our own experience can give us.[3]

With this perspective, it makes sense that Christians walk out of step and out of time with mainstream culture. We don't have to keep up with the whims and fads of advertising or the latest 'progressive' thinking or a political correctness that seeks to silence the gospel and create a beige uniformity of beliefs. Rather than being swept along by the crowd and the things that 'everyone' is saying, believing and doing, we have a choice. That choice is outworked by how closely we choose to follow Jesus. We become lost on a walk like we become lost in life when we refuse to take time to stop and consider where the good way is.

'Stand at the crossroads and look;
ask for the ancient paths,
ask where the good way is, and walk in it,
and you will find rest for your souls.'
(Jeremiah 6.16)

There are some crossroads at which we must be prepared to wait and assess the options. Will this road lead me into all that God has for me? Does it fit with who I am called to be? Is it ancient? Is it good? Waiting is an act of defiance. It is rebellion to the advertisers and the moneymakers who want us to be carried along unthinkingly. We are those who wait on God to ask which way to walk; we don't go along with the crowd and the status quo. Jesus put it another way: he described it as the narrow way (see Matthew 7.14, MEV). Jesus offended then and he offends us now when he says that 'there are few who find it'. Will you find it? Will you walk in it?

Friends on the road

Our support team would meet us at arranged rendezvous places every five to seven miles and provide pit stops that would refuel and replenish the increasingly flagging energy levels. After 15 miles we were approaching Windsor, and as we rounded a corner the castle and its grounds came into view. A patch of grass outside Windsor Castle was the perfect resting point for a fish and chip supper and an opportunity to change socks and compare blisters. If we were in danger of enjoying the rest too much, we needn't have worried – the Queen's Security, concerned at the size of the group and its proximity to Her Majesty, politely moved us on as the last few chips were being devoured. We were 15 miles down, with 35 to go.

One of the joys of walking is being able to walk with others. Walking on the towpath allowed for conversations to meander like the river, going with the flow and sometimes taking surprising turns. In pairs or small groups we could explore ideas and put the world to rights, we could move from idle chit-chat to places of vulnerability and openness. On the road of life we learn to walk with each other and we hear one another's hopes and dreams, fears and failures, and accept one another for who we are. We get to see more of the real person, see the potential and call out the gold; we also get to respond to the pain. When we walk with each other we meet in a deeper way; through walking and talking we learn to recognize Christ in each other. Like the disciples on the road to Emmaus, we meet Christ on the road.

We are made for relationships. Friends who care enough about us will speak truth to us even when it is uncomfortable and risks offence. I know that as I get older I want my friends to sharpen me and say the things that I need to hear, the things that are easier to hear from a friend than from a stranger or not at all. Survival is possible on our own, but we are made for more. And the only way to cultivate these sorts of championing friendships is to be the friend you want to have. A friend who takes the time to ask you how you are doing and really wants to know. A friend who is sufficiently 'other'-focused that he or she notices the subtleties of your mood. A friend who is interested enough to enquire whether there is anything else going on and is ready to share the burden and take a stand. A friend who cares and takes the initiative to walk and talk, and to pray and invite God to join the journey. A friend who will encourage you to be true to your calling, to keep following Jesus and walking with him. You will probably count these sorts of friends on one hand during your entire life. Let me encourage you to choose your friends carefully and to be the friend you want to have.

Awkward steps

Our walk is a shared walk. How I walk affects your walk and how you walk affects my walk. In Christ we are part of the same body and are called to walk with those who are very different from ourselves. It is one of the reasons why being part of a church community is non-negotiable for a Christian. It is impossible to live the Christian life effectively without the Church, and it is in the huge diversity of God's people that we find Christ. We find Christ when we learn to appreciate one another, when we tread on each other's toes and have to forgive one another, when we disagree and still love one another. And it is through our love-charged inter-actions that others will see Christ in us.

> 'It is impossible to live the Christian life
> effectively without the Church, and it is in the
> huge diversity of God's people that we find
> Christ.'

As well as walking with those close to us, walking well with those who don't share our perspectives and theological emphasis requires a maturity that refuses to belittle, shame, divide or accuse. It is delusional to think that we can slander, moan about or disown another part of the Church with-out it having a negative impact on us or the wider Church. Careless and cutting comments from one part of the Church to another is like spiritual self-harm: we wound ourselves and we wound Christ. We must model how to walk together, share with one another, bear with one another, rejoice with one another, mourn with one another, love one another and forgive one another. Jesus died so that we could be one in

Christ, and we are required to die to the things that would cause any division to that oneness. When we walk in unity, God releases his blessing, and true unity will always come at a personal cost and will always command a corporate blessing.

Walking through the night

As the walk progressed, forgiveness was definitely needed towards the person who had suggested walking 50 miles non-stop! A further 15 miles on and the sun had long since gone to bed, the night air was cool and the moon cast shadows as our eyes adjusted. Walking was now a conscious endeavour, conversations and external noise decreased and the sound of our footsteps increased. Occasionally our foot-fall would synchronize to a rhythmic chant and the beat of crisp steps could be heard. We were an increasingly small platoon marching for a kingdom cause. Our initial squad of 15 had been whittled down to eight. It was becoming a busy night for Matt and Phil on the support team as their van filled up with fallen comrades.

Sleep is what normally dominates our night-time; however, there are times and seasons when the night is where we need to contend, wrestle and persevere. It was in the night that Samuel heard God calling to him (1 Samuel 3), it was a night of wrestling that left Jacob walking with a limp (Genesis 32.22–32), it was a night-time prayer and worship session that led to a prison break for Paul and Silas (Acts 16.25–36), and it was a night of prayer and waiting on God the Father before Jesus called his disciples (Luke 6.12–13). Occasionally we may voluntarily persevere through the night; more often we are troubled by thoughts that disturb our sleep and keep us awake.

The night-time is often when God grabs our attention in a different way. Henri Nouwen shares that:

> much real prayer of communion takes place in the night, in the night of faith, in the darkness that comes upon us because the light of God is so great that it blinds us and makes our heart and mind unable to grasp what we are learning.[4]

Some things can only be learned at night.

Persevering through the night is both a reality and a metaphor for how we choose to keep walking and not give up. In the darkness there are lessons to be learned, battles to be faced and treasures to be found. The question is not whether the setbacks will come. The Bible leaves us in no doubt that troubles will come. Isaiah 43.2 reads, 'I will be with you; and when you pass through the rivers, they will not sweep over you. When you walk through the fire, you will not be burned; the flames will not set you ablaze.' It is comforting to know that God will be with us. However, we need to notice that the word the prophet uses in this passage is not 'if' but 'when' we encounter hardship. The question is, will we trust God in these moments? Will we hold on to his hand in walking out our calling through whatever season we find ourselves in?

*'Persevering through the night is both a reality
and a metaphor for how we choose to keep
walking and not give up. In the darkness there*

*are lessons to be learned, battles to be faced
and treasures to be found.'*

Your calling will be tested. The darkness distorts reality; nightmares don't happen in the day. When we are tired, our thinking can become like a runaway train that affects our mental health, emotions and sense of peace. Fears like to roam in the dark. It is the light that exposes them for what they are: the small mouse that casts a 12-foot shadow on the wall and scares the elephant.

To persevere through dark nights and dark thoughts takes courage. Jesus is with you in them and calls you on. Keep moving because there is freedom on the other side, and the things that plagued you in the past won't plague you in the future. Persevering in the dark is a great act of trust: we commit back to God all that we can't control, all that troubles us, all that confuses us, and we keep going. The night may be long at times, but sooner or later day will break – with new mercy and new grace we keep walking in response to God's calling.

Grace and grit

The night of non-stop walking took its toll and only five of the team survived to see dawn break. Bruised, blistered and bleeding feet; sore, aching and tired legs had diminished our numbers. Conversation had given way to silence; walking was now deliberate, laboured and painful. Each surviving pilgrim now had a distinct and slightly unnatural walking style, stepping gingerly in an attempt to cushion bruised soles as the step count approached six figures. It required concentration. It required willpower.

So much of life is about persevering through pain and discomfort. Keeping going requires grace and grit. Indeed, the more deeply we commit to engaging in God's mission to the world, the grittier life will become. It will also yield more treasure and beauty than we could have imagined. Pearls are formed when a piece of sand or grit becomes trapped in the shell of an oyster. The grit is an irritant and an inconvenience, but it isn't spat out; rather it is embraced and transformed. Over time the grit becomes less abrasive and irritating because the oyster slowly coats it in mother-of-pearl. Slowly and surely a beautiful pearl is born.

Like most metaphors for maturity, it can be dismissed all too quickly – our feeling brain kicks in and screams, 'This is uncomfortable and I don't like it!' If we are prepared to engage a little longer and allow our thinking brain to take over, the concept begins to lose its sense of threat. The things that become powerful and living in us are the things that we have fought for and embraced. The foolish, ugly, painful parts we submit to Christ and one another slowly and surely become coated in layers of grace. They become not only gifts for ourselves, but also gifts that we get to give away generously and abundantly.

When we accept that this is the case, we can stop using sticky plasters for wounds that require surgery. We can exchange false comforts for transformative conversations and disciplines. We can stop living in denial and face reality, confident that with God nothing is too dark, too broken or too far gone. With God, there is always a way, and he will walk with us down that path. Speaking to both our suffering and our perseverance, Paul encourages the church in Corinth with these words:

Therefore we do not lose heart. Though outwardly we are wasting away, yet inwardly we are being renewed day by day. For our light and momentary troubles are achieving for us an eternal glory that far outweighs them all. So we fix our eyes not on what is seen, but on what is unseen, since what is seen is temporary, but what is unseen is eternal.
(2 Corinthians 4.16–18)

With our eyes fixed on Christ we find hope and meaning in the most hopeless and meaningless places.

What else keeps you going? What keeps you putting one foot in front of the other through life's ups and downs? Our walk needs to be full of purpose, and that purpose is fuelled by godly ambition. Ambition is neither good nor bad, but it is essential if we are to walk with perseverance. Our ambition seems to fall into one of two categories – making a name for ourselves or making a way for God. Sometimes the line feels blurred, but a healthy ambition is one that is submitted to God. And God wants us to be ambitious for him, to live big and to outwork the high calling that he has placed in each one of us.

> 'What else keeps you going? What keeps you putting one foot in front of the other through life's ups and downs? Our walk needs to be full of purpose, and that purpose is fuelled by godly ambition.'

An epic poem

Jesus was the most ambitious man who has ever lived: saving humanity and setting the cosmos straight is no small dream. And Christ made us to participate in this divine dream and become more aware of Christ's ambition for our lives: 'For we are His workmanship, created in Christ Jesus for good works, which God prepared beforehand that we should walk in them' (Ephesians 2.10, NKJV).

These are no idle words of Paul. They declare that when God made us, he made us the pinnacle of creation that bears his image. Paul chose the Greek word *poiema*, from which we get our English word 'poem', to describe God's workmanship. We are his creative masterpiece, we are his priceless work of art, we are his epic poem, crafted to be read by the world so that others too will learn to walk with God. Where we lack ambition, Christ has ambition for us – we are made for good works. Without ambition, passivity replaces passion. We stop walking and become armchair commentators on the life we are no longer participating in. When Jesus comes into our lives, he ignites us with a passion and purpose that ejects us off the couch and into a God adventure.

What is so remarkable about the ambition of Jesus is the way he outworked it. He reframed ambition away from power and prestige to embody the posture and the person of a servant:

> Rather, he made himself nothing
> by taking the very nature of a servant,
> being made in human likeness.
> (Philippians 2.7)

The Bible starts with an account of humanity being formed in God's likeness. The start of the New Testament then describes God being formed in human likeness. The Christmas story split time in two, and 2,000 years later it fills us with wonder and expectation. We must conclude that God really valued what he had made. Could God pay humanity a greater compliment than becoming like us? If we were ever in doubt about how much God loves us, how highly he prizes us, then the self-emptying act of becoming like us is the start of a new covenant. A more permanent and committed act towards humanity is not conceivable.

'When we talk about walking in our calling,
we are talking about servanthood.'

According to Jesus, the greatest leaders are the greatest servants: 'But not so with you. Rather, let the greatest among you become as the youngest, and the leader as one who serves' (Luke 22.26, ESV). When we talk about walking in our calling, we are talking about servanthood.

When I think about where my calling in God began to be formed, it was when I began serving people: I started serving Ness and getting behind what she was doing with church and students. My vision and passion for church and students grew and developed as I served Ness's vision for them. Then I started serving Roger Ellis in his wider vision for church and students, and very quickly it began to feel like my own. Christ became flesh and blood to show us how to serve God, and we become alive when we have 'skin in the game'. We become more fully alive when this piece of art, poetry, workmanship gets to work.

In a sense, our individual calling doesn't exist; it is God's calling on our lives that we respond to, and we often discover it by laying down our personal agenda and serving other people. Servanthood unlocks true identity and calling. The outworking is often far more challenging and demanding than we could ever have imagined, and perseverance deepens our conviction of God's calling.

Have you ever considered that the people and places where you are now serving and working are a doorway to your calling? Ask God to give you his perspective. In our fast-moving culture, it can be all too easy to overlook where God has us now in favour of where we want him to take us. Don't be too hasty to move on from jobs that feel boring and mundane or be reluctant to take a job that isn't in your sweet spot. What else does God want to teach you right where you are? Your calling is tested and sharpened through workplace environments, persevering with revision, making deadlines and being good news to those around you. Lessons learned and skills gained in one environment can be transferred to and bear fruit in another.

> 'In our fast-moving culture, it can be all too
> easy to overlook where God has us now in
> favour of where we want him to take us.'

The final steps

The last five miles were hard. Each step was felt and earned; it had a physical price. Our bodies were counting the cost of the decision to walk such a distance. We were blistered and bloodied from the ordeal, our smaller walking pilgrimage reflecting something of our larger life pilgrimage.

Life, like this sponsored walk, gives us many opportunities and excuses to stop, to give up or to quit. There have been times where quitting Fusion, Open Heaven or even faith would have felt like an easier option. Some tasks have felt too hard, too big; some life events have been so overwhelming and disappointing, and to keep going has felt like risking more pain and more disappointment. However, it is the very act of walking and keeping going that is transformational, and that is something we can't afford to give up on. The change that comes through trial and challenge does not come any other way. It is the way of Jesus, it is the way of the cross and it is God's way for us and for his will to be done on earth.

At the finish line, our support team and some of our fallen comrades cheered and clapped as Luke, Miriam, Gemma and I hobbled past them. We'd been walking for just over 19 hours and learned a little more about ourselves, our friends and our limits. Miriam, Luke and I were raising money but it went deeper than that. The simple steps of walking changed how we saw ourselves and the things God had called us to. The struggle in the final miles, the willpower needed when the body was screaming pain and tiredness, was also fuelling a deeper calling.

How much will you really give of yourself to see your dream and vision come about? Our shared experience created a common and deeper bond for what we believed we could achieve together. In mainstream culture, where commitment is undervalued, it would lead to us having conversations around what it would look like for all of us to commit the next ten years of our life to this cause. Persevering together, although still hugely challenging, is far easier than persevering alone.

We walk undefended, embracing misunderstanding. We walk secretly, content to keep some of our achievements just between us and God. We walk openly, ready for others to walk alongside. We walk humbly, adopting the nature of a servant. We walk with perseverance, pushing through walls and pain barriers. We walk with assurance, knowing that the one who invited us to walk is faithful and will see that we reach the finish line. We walk out our salvation with fear and trembling, conscious of the enormous price that was paid. We walk because we've been captivated by beauty beyond words and it compels our next step. We walk out of time with the culture and in time with God. We walk because walking is better than sitting down. We walk along ancient paths and forge new ones. We walk purposefully, our eyes on the one we follow, and we walk with hope, because one day it will all be worth it.

'Twenty years from now you will be more disappointed by the things you didn't do than by the ones you did do. So throw off the bowlines. Sail away from the safe harbour. Catch the trade winds in your sails. Explore. Dream. Discover.'

MARK TWAIN

8

Calling and adventure:
Escape and Pray

It's 3 a.m. and my alarm wakes me with a start. Adrenaline kills my momentary disorientation as I remember that today is the day: I am going on a prayer adventure. Within 20 minutes I'm making my way to Luton airport, feeling a little nervous about the trip. I am travelling with a student called Jack, but neither one of us knows where we are going.

We are one of 35 teams participating in an experimental mission idea called Escape and Pray.[1] Teams of two, three or four students have registered their passport details and paid a £100 fee to Fusion and in return have been asked to be at a UK airport on a specific date and at a specific time. Fusion has provided the equivalent of 20 euros each to survive on and a dirtproof black T-shirt with Escape&Pray emblazoned across the front. Our instructions are simple: once at the airport we are to open the shiny orange envelope we've been asked to bring along, revealing our destination and containing challenges to do along the way.

Not every adventure has to do with calling (and we all have our own definition of what constitutes an adventure!). However, when you pursue God's calling, I can guarantee that you will find yourself caught up in a much bigger God adventure than any you could plan on your own. Jack and I were about to be reminded of just that.

> *'When you pursue God's calling, I can*
> *guarantee that you will find yourself caught up*
> *in a much bigger God adventure than any you*
> *could plan on your own.'*

An adventure begins

With our overnight bags, passports and the envelope in hand, Jack and I found ourselves almost carried to Departures by the football-sized crowd eager to get away and breathing a similar air of expectation to that provided by any Cup Final. Unlike them, however, we still didn't know where we were going. Jack's hands were trembling with excitement as he fumbled to unstick the super-strong glue, now the only thing in the way of what had been weeks of waiting to find out where we were going. Eventually he managed to prise open the stubborn barrier and slid out a piece of paper with one word on it: *Reykjavik*.

Neither of us had ever been to Iceland, and instantly we were bombarding each other with questions: What is the weather like? Have we brought the right clothes? Do we know anyone there? What on earth do we do now? We paused to pray and commit our trip and the next 48 hours to God – after all, that's what this adventure was all about.

A relatively short time later, we arrived in Iceland. Within a nation of 323,000 people we were now more than 30 miles from the main population centre and capital city of Reykjavik.

'Jack, is there anything else in that envelope that will help us get to Reykjavik?' I asked.

'Nor,' replied Jack in his strong Yorkshire accent.

We walked out of the airport into a small car park.

'I think we are going to have to hitchhike. Let's get asking some people,' I suggested, and then promptly walked off to see if I could find a lift as Jack ripped page after page out of his A5 journal trying repeatedly to spell Reykjavik correctly and attempting to fit all the letters on one page. Jack's sign was not pretty, but it worked! Within ten minutes, two friendly Icelandic 'angels' called Hilder and Birna were kindly offering us a lift to the capital. As we began to motor through the arid, desert-like landscape, Jack turned to me and said, 'I've never done anything like this before,' his eyes glinting with an aliveness that belied his chilled-out Yorkshire demeanour.

'Travelling paths we have never taken before causes an inner displacement, sometimes permanent, that switches us on to more of the life and longing God has for us.'

Jack's comment captured something of the spirit of Escape and Pray. There is longing for adventure – in a variety of forms – in everyone. On the surface, Escape and Pray is about prayer: praying for transformation; praying for people; praying that whole universities, cities and nations will awaken to the call of God. It is also about personal awakening. In going somewhere different, where we will most probably experience and do things we have never done before, we are loosing creativity, curiosity and wonder into our scheduled and screen-filled worlds. Travelling paths we have never taken before causes an inner displacement, sometimes permanent, that switches us on to more of the life and longing God has for us.

Fear of freedom

'It is for freedom that Christ has set us free' (Galatians 5.1), and yet the lives of young and old are increasingly shackled by fear. Fear that has been passed down to us by our parents and our education, and fear that we have picked up in the many experiences we have been through ourselves or witnessed on our phones, televisions and computer screens. Our appetite for adventure is still there, but it is often buried beneath a rubbish dump of lies and fears.

I recently read an article titled 'How Children Lost the Right to Roam in Four Generations'.[2] It captured something of the cultural change that is having a severe impact on our freedom. It tells the story of George Thomas who, when he was eight years old, walked everywhere. The year was 1926 and he would regularly walk six miles to his favourite fishing haunt without adult supervision. Fast forward nearly 100 years and George Thomas's eight-year-old great-grandson Edward enjoys none of that freedom. He is driven the few minutes it takes to get to school, is taken by car to a safe place to ride his bike and can roam no more than 200 yards from home. In fact, 200 yards now seems excessively risky for most. A few years ago, I was speaking to a group of students and twenty-somethings, and one young man confessed to never having been allowed to roam more than 15 yards from home. I am not suggesting we return to the past. I do, however, think we should reflect more on what impact modern life is having on us – specifically, the impact of media on our well-being and attitude to risk.

Media exposes people to an ocean of stories, ideas, images and possibilities. We are bombarded with advertising and made aware of the latest happenings from right across the globe. We are the most informed generation ever, *but is all this information doing us any good?* It is good to pray for those we see suffering on our television screens, but are we really designed to see that amount of distress in our lifetime? Previous generations were exposed to less and seemed to be less fearful and anxious. How do you filter what you consume? What would a healthier media diet look and feel like? And why does it really matter?

The inner adventure

The outer adventure without the inner adventure will very likely lead to empty hedonism. It is the inner adventure that gives the outer adventure roots and context. The inner adventure is our pursuit after God; it is wild and treacherous and it is also calm and reassuring. It holds the keys to our identity and contentment and is at the heart of our calling to be a disciple.

> *'The outer adventure without the inner adventure will very likely lead to empty hedonism. It is the inner adventure that gives the outer adventure roots and context. The inner adventure is our pursuit after God.'*

These words from A. W. Tozer summarize why the inner adventure really matters: 'What comes into our minds when we think about God is the most important thing about us.'[3] Thoughts can be like runaway trains that affect not only our mental health but also our spiritual health. Many refer to this inner adventure as spiritual formation and, as I have mentioned, it takes place in every season of life – indeed, every moment of life. It is what God is forming in you as you co-operate with his work in your life, even as you read this book!

We can begin to participate more fully with the inner adventure when we realize that our yearning and longing for more cannot be filled by external entertainment. Yet our desires are so deep and so real that it feels as though they could be. Our bodies, full of energy, hormones and sex drive, are clearly made for more than the sofa and the screen. This very aliveness is God breathed and is the vision of God.[4]

If the inner adventure is shut down or ignored or simply deemed to be too demanding, then everything points towards the outward or the appearance thereof. In our celebrity-obsessed culture, with social media platforms providing numerous peepholes into people's lives, a whole generation is in danger of living vicariously. A vicarious life is simply one that is experienced in the imagination through the feelings or actions of another person. We end up living in our heads. Professor Ken Robinson, describing his academic friends, jokes that 'they use their bodies merely as a transport system for their heads'.[5] This is a brutal and damning indictment compared to the life that God has for us.

Much of the online world of computer games and social media is pure fantasy, and that fantasy becomes a substitute for adventure. Lots of it, if left without boundaries and thoughtful engagement, is obsessive and addictive and becomes a substitute for passion. And yet adventure and passion is what the Holy Spirit wants to fuel in our lives, because we are made for more. When the inward adventure is ignited with the life of God, the outward adventure is a natural consequence.

Research shows that excessive 'screen time' is damaging to mental and physical health.[6] This diminishes our humanity and our ability to both live out and recognize our calling. An unbalanced diet of computer games and social media creates unhealthy addictions and obsessions. I notice it in myself. Whether it is long hours of passivity indoors, the constant distraction from notifications or the thoughtless addiction to checking our phones, you and I can become slaves to a much smaller life than God has for us. We then struggle to be present with ourselves, let alone anyone else, and yet at the same time we are yearning to be present in God's presence.

God is calling us into his much bigger and much more fulfilling life, and we can choose how we participate. This is too important to ignore. Start the detox now. Turn off notifications, remove social media apps, even lock your phone in a drawer, unsubscribe from Netflix, and allow your body and mind to breathe again. Reclaim your imagination and creativity; it has been quietly suffocating in the name of entertainment.

My hero

Growing up, we all have our heroes. For me, right near the top of that list is my grandpa. For my entire childhood he lived close by with my granny, and the short, five-mile journey to their house was always exciting. He had built it himself before *Grand Designs* and building your own house was popular. It was situated near the top of a hill on the edge of the Peak District surrounded by fields. Sometimes I would stay there with my brother James for a few days at a time, and this would allow James and me to explore and create our own mini adventures. However, it was time with my grandpa that I relished most. I always found him engaging, his stories and many talents stretching my horizons; I loved him dearly.

It came as a surprise to me, therefore, that on one Sunday afternoon in my mid-teens he began to share how he was living with some regret. The football match we had been watching on television together soon became irrelevant as he continued to disclose how he felt he hadn't done anything with his life. I was shocked – this was my grandpa, whom I admired for so many reasons. He had been faithfully married for more than 50 years. He was a man of faith and a successful businessman. I loved the fact he had been on the books of Manchester City in the 1920s – my beloved football team. He had led one of the largest Crusaders groups in the country in south Manchester, attracting more than 300 boys for weekly Bible study. He had lived through two World Wars, had been conscripted for the Second World War and had been away for five years. The only war stories he shared were of going fishing with hand grenades and needing to steal a motorbike for an emergency. I only found out after he died that he had been awarded three bravery medals – no one knew. He was a humble, generous and kind man.

At the time I was taken aback and did my best to cheer him up, a role I wasn't used to playing. His wasn't a viewpoint I could shift; he'd been reflecting on his 79 years and this was his conclusion. I was shocked then; I am less shocked now.

I sometimes imagine myself as an 80-year-old and ponder whether I too would regret not being bolder and braver in my approach to life. If I had a chance to do it all again, what would I do differently?

This conversation with my grandpa reminded me of a sociological study that Dr Anthony Campolo talks about in which 50 people over the age of 95 were asked one question: 'If you could live your life over again, what would you do differently?'[7] The open-ended question was met with a multiplicity of answers from the respondents. However, three conclusions emerged that dominate the results of the study:

- If we had to do it over again, we would reflect more.
- If we had to do it over again, we would risk more.
- If we had to do it over again, we would do more things that would live on after we are dead.

For these participants, the first televisions would not have arrived in their homes until they were in their sixties. The world they grew up in had far fewer distractions than we have today, and yet this study reveals a need to take more time out to reflect. Instead of getting swept along by the everyday tasks, chores and demands, they would have created more time to contemplate the really important things.

'Do you recognize the moments when you are fully alive? Does that affect what you give your time to?'

Reflecting on life and the life God has for us and how we participate fully requires discipline. Time slips by; life slips by. Do you recognize the moments when you are fully alive? Does that affect what you give your time to?

Despite living through the massive changes of the twentieth century, the participants' answers reveal an unfulfilled need for adventure. They reflect that they played their lives too safe and that, looking back, the risks they did take didn't seem all that risky. I grew up as part of the generation with only three television channels and I used to watch a television programme ironically called *Why Don't You Just Switch Off Your Television Set and Go Out and Do Something Less Boring Instead?* For many people born in the last few decades, by the time they are 70 they will have spent ten years watching screens for entertainment. If this study were to be done again 50 years from now and if you could do life over again, I wonder whether you would turn off the phone and television more.

Finally, the participants desired their lives to have a lasting impact on future generations – a provocative insight that can only be seen so clearly from the vantage point of old age. Up until this later life stage we mainly spend our energy on ourselves and our immediate families. It is legacy thinking that challenges our motives in how we live and what we live for. The choices we make now have repercussions. Will future generations thank us for those choices? After we die, what stories might people tell, not only about the difference our lives made, but also about what we fought for, stood for and ultimately died for?

Pilgrims, not tourists

On the road to Reykjavik, conversation flowed with Hilder and Birna as we explained the strange quest we were on and asked many questions about this nation we knew very little about. I got used to translating a little of Jack's Yorkshire into English, something that would serve us well during our trip. Hilder and Birna were proud of their nation and, like many we were to meet, open to spirituality, but were disillusioned and frustrated by the state church. A few miles into our journey, they insisted on a quick detour to show us the blue lagoon, a stunning hot spring nestled atmospherically between the dramatic volcanic rocks. This was the ultimate wild swim location and a place to come back to on a later visit. As Jack and I breathed in the beauty of the place, we reminded ourselves that in this land of fire and ice we were pilgrims, not tourists. Jim Forest found words that defined the essence of our trip:

> Pilgrimage – whether the sort that involves going long distances to unfamiliar lands or simply being aware of ordinary life as a cradle-to-the-grave pilgrimage – is an invitation to become a person capable of seeing interruptions, most of all those involving the urgent need of others, as heaven sent opportunities that have the potential of bringing us closer to the Kingdom of God. Whether washing dishes in the kitchen or walking to Jerusalem, life is learning to see interruptions as God's plan for the day rather than one's own plan, and thus to live in God's time rather than clock time.[8]

*'The call of God reverberates, resonates and
echoes in the ordinariness of daily life and can
easily be overlooked.'*

It is so easy to be consumed with our own plans, whether at work or at home, going to the gym, a party or even a wedding. We have our agendas in work, rest and play, and interruptions inconvenience us and disrupt us – but they don't have to. They can, if we choose to embrace them, transform barren ground and frustration into fertile ground for growth in God and portals for his presence to be experienced. God is not a compartment in our lives, and going to church meetings is not a lifestyle choice – and maybe, just maybe, interruptions are not interruptions at all, but invitations to participate in the extravagant life that Jesus promises us. The call of God reverberates, resonates and echoes in the ordinariness of daily life and can easily be overlooked.

Excuse me, Son

The Son of God was not immune to interruptions. On the contrary, those moments, it seems, are where some of his best-remembered work happened. His ministry started with an interruption. In John 2 Jesus is at a wedding. It's downtime, an opportunity to hang out, to chat and celebrate. Initially, it seems that Jesus is resistant to the interruption from his mum about a shortage of wine. 'It's not my problem or yours,' is his initial reply. However, his mother's intuition is persistent, and the stage is set for heaven to break in.

Jesus' ministry starts with the most extravagant miracle, a sign that when he declares that he offers life to the full, he means it. The equivalent of as many as 900 bottles of top-quality wine is created in a moment. Enough to more than satisfy the wedding guests, but not enough for a thirsty world: that would require a different sort of wine.

It is this wine that Jesus is remembered for. His earthly ministry was one of being continually poured out for the sake of others. The cup of suffering he embraced on the cross became the doorway to true communion and a ritual of remembrance in which all his future followers would be invited to regularly participate.

Often, the most fascinating and interesting stories come as a result of being inconvenienced. Two thousand years later, this story is still being told and enacted as Christians break bread and drink wine in gatherings small and large, in homes and auditoriums around the world. Interruptions open doors for stories, adventures and miracles.

How we differentiate between an interruption in God's time and merely an inconvenience to our clock time has much to do with what we anticipate. We will recognize more readily that which we have been focusing on or looking for. If you or your family have ever bought a car, a peculiar thing happens. All of a sudden that model of car is everywhere. Have they increased? No, but your awareness of them has. Your focus and gaze have been trained to recognize the car you have spent the most time looking at. It is similar with the voice and presence of God: when Jesus becomes a focus in our lives, he can then be recognized in all kinds of people and places, irritations and interruptions.

Beach mission

Escape and Pray in Iceland was one long interruption. We had little agenda and lots of time to listen to anyone who wanted to talk. One of our more unusual meetings was in a communal hot tub. Let me explain!

Nauthólsvík Geothermal Beach was just a few miles' walk from the centre of Reykjavik. After speaking with a number of locals, Jack and I decided it was a place to visit. The beach is human-made and boasts two giant hot tubs heated by the natural hot springs. The sea temperature around Reykjavik was a chilly 8°C. A recent obsession with wild swimming had ensured that swimming shorts were packed in the hope that an opportunity might arise. Jack and I opted for the long, rectangular hot tub.

'I've never done anything like this before,' chimed Jack. A phrase that was now well worn.

We soon engaged in more conversations, this time with a couple of recent students, Jónas and Daniel, whose stories moved us.

Our visit in June allowed us to experience the phenomenon known as the 'midnight sun', where the night-time hours bestow a lingering twilight – it never goes dark. In contrast, the deep midwinter days hardly light up, and this outer darkness is mirrored in the lives of many of Iceland's young people. Jónas and Daniel were graduates of the University of Reykjavik and they were also recovering alcoholics. The dark days had been a contributing factor in depression for both young men, and alcohol was what they had turned to.

Iceland as a nation has a strange relationship with alcohol. Prohibition in the country went into effect in 1915 and lasted until 1 March 1989. This day is now celebrated by many as 'Beer Day'.

This is not a day that Jónas and Daniel celebrated. They were getting their young lives back on track, lives that multiple beer days had nearly destroyed. Jack and I shared our journey, our conviction to pray, our hope in Jesus and a gentle challenge for them to explore faith. There was no baptism in the hot tub that day, but seeds were sown and silent prayers were prayed.

Jónas and Daniel had a more direct challenge for us: to climb out of the hot tub and into the North Atlantic Sea. Challenge accepted.

Authentic community

Our 48-hour escape to Iceland coincided with a Sunday and we wanted to connect with a church to pray, to share our story and to bless what God was doing in Iceland. A little bit of research led us to Fíladelfía, an international church that met in the afternoon in the centre of Reykjavik. This was an eclectic gathering of around 30 people of different nationalities, different backgrounds and different walks of life. It was unpolished, a little clunky at times, and refreshingly real and authentic – it was church.

It is a privilege to travel to another part of the world and find home because we find people who share our faith in Christ. Fíladelfía was warm and welcoming, and after worshipping and praying together there was time to get to know people and to share stories and hopes and dreams of what God had in store for this beautiful nation.

Experiences of church communities like this are special, and in our consumer culture they are also a provocation and reminder of what church is really all about. Other than through Jesus, there was very little chance that this group of people would ever be in the same room. Our commonality was found in Christ, and friendship was instant because we recognized Christ in each other. The Christians we met hadn't shopped around for their favourite music style for worship or a meeting that offered the best Bible teaching. From what we could see, being a Christian in Iceland was not a consumer activity; it was about being committed to journeying with God's people and making a contribution.

Consumer church is at odds with adventurous faith. We don't grow and mature by consuming more of our preferred content in a package and style that we find enjoyable. We grow in seasons and situations that are abrasive, uncomfortable and risky. It is our approach and attitude to church that determines whether we are treating gathering with God's people as a consumer or an entertaining experience or making our contribution to building the body of Christ.

> *'Consumer church is at odds with adventurous faith. We don't grow and mature by consuming more of our preferred content in a package and style that we find enjoyable. We grow in seasons and situations that are abrasive, uncomfortable and risky.'*

Prayer and paradoxes

Finding accommodation can be one of the most challenging aspects of an Escape and Pray adventure, and it is a discipline not to dominate prayers with our needs and to keep our attention focused outwards. Hospitality can't be demanded; it has to be offered. The church building that Fíladelfía uses is often on offer to pilgrims to use for a night. However, the pastor was away and so we were encouraged to seek out the Salvation Army hostel in downtown Reykjavik. This proved to be a fantastic base from which to walk and pray.

Our short escape to Iceland was nearly done, and before leaving we had time to visit the University of Reykjavik. No Escape and Pray is complete without time and space to pray for all that God wants to do in the hearts and minds of students. I think it is common that the older a person becomes, the greater the desire to invest in future generations. This investment was a prayer deposit. A prayer that in Iceland and in the University of Reykjavik God's kingdom would come and his will would be done; that young men and women would get a glimpse of the goodness of God and determine to live obediently and faithfully for him; that the church here would not be like the 'lukewarm' church in Laodicea (see Revelation 3.14–16), but be marked by fire or ice.

Every time we ventured in and out of the Salvation Army hostel our journey was interrupted for 10 to 15 minutes as we listened to the stories of Albert, the friendly warden. He hailed from the wilder western isles of Iceland, and with a very straight face would tell tales of his boyhood adventures, playing with elves and Icelandic magic and folklore.

Iceland is full of paradoxes, faith and folklore; it is a landscape that consists of volcanoes and snow, fire and ice. Behind the stunning natural beauty lie some confusing contradictions. According to a 2015 study, Iceland tops the global list for antidepressant consumption per capita.[9] If you're not sure how that fits with being ranked the world's third-happiest nation in 2017,[10] you're not alone. Eighty-five per cent of Iceland's inhabitants are supposedly Christians, and yet Iceland is considered the world's sixth most atheistic nation.[11] On this second point, it is the existence of the

Lutheran State Church that claims this level of membership; our conversations on the streets backed up a broad rejection of institutionalized religion and it felt as though atheism was more of a protest than a fixed position. I had huge sympathy with many I met who shared this viewpoint: Jesus never offered institutionalized religion; he offered relationship. Friendship and faith were at the heart of Christ's invitation to a full and free life.

Like Iceland itself, a life of following Jesus can be full of paradoxes. On the one hand, Jesus says that he has 'come that they may have life, and have it to the full' (John 10.10). On the other hand, he says, 'You will have suffering in this world. Be courageous! I have conquered the world' (John 16.33, HCSB). In responding to the call of God, we start to participate in a huge God adventure – life to the full. We also engage in a spiritual battle. The brokenness in our world because of sin and a common adversary (Satan) means we will have adversity – we will suffer. In other words, we are called into a life of adventure and adversity.

Adventure and adversity. These two promises can seem like complete opposites. How can I have life to the full and be subject to suffering at the same time? As I try to live this tension, I imagine myself with arms open wide, feeling stretched as I try to keep hold of both promises. It is deeply uncomfortable and seemingly untenable in my own strength. Indeed, it seems that much of the Church in the West has let go of one or the other. For a smaller percentage, all they can see is suffering, and they feel guilty for identifying with anything extravagant or abundant. For a larger percentage, all suffering is to be resisted, and life to the full means that any negative emotions and difficulties are not of God.

> '*Adventure and adversity. These two promises*
> *can seem like complete opposites. How can I*
> *have life to the full and be subject to suffering*
> *at the same time?*'

Holding on to one and not the other could be a very valid argument if it weren't the Son of God making these promises. Jesus shows us how to live the tension. Jesus teaches me that as I surrender to the tension, I find my arms are pulled towards each other and the palms of my hands come together to form a new posture. The tension remains, and it is prayer that makes it bearable and lightens the load.

We can bring our arms together only because on the cross Jesus kept his arms stretched out. Christ bore it all, made a way for us and invites us to join in, picking up our cross daily to share in his suffering, that we might also share in his glory (Romans 8.17).

Some things Jesus said and did make him easy to follow. There are other things that make it much harder. In taking a look at how the early disciples were called and how they responded, we can learn how to participate better in the life, calling and faith adventure God has for us – even when the invitation isn't particularly attractive.

Interruptions and calling

Luke 5 starts with a story of Jesus getting his feet wet – or so it would seem. The crowd are pressing in on him – everyone wants a selfie – and Jesus is having to deal with his newfound celebrity status. Meanwhile, there are a few guys just getting on with their work. They are fishermen, and one of the most important skills of fishermen is making and mending nets. They fish at night, and then the nets, which are made of linen, have to be carefully cleaned and dried each day, or they will quickly rot and wear out.

As Jesus is now about to get very wet, he interrupts a fisherman called Simon to ask if he can borrow his boat and be given a little push away from the shore. A short while later, after Jesus has spoken to the crowds, he interrupts Simon again with a much more demanding request: to go fishing again, this time in the deeper water.

To you and me this might seem reasonable – after all, Simon is a fisherman, so no big deal, right? The response of Simon is telling – he is tired and down, he caught nothing last night and he has just finished cleaning his nets for the coming night's fishing. He probably just wants an afternoon nap – this is an interruption he can do without. I can imagine him saying, 'Jesus, you're a carpenter and you make a fantastic table but you don't know anything about fishing. This isn't the right time of day to fish; our nets are white linen and are for night fishing. The fish will see them a mile away. No one has ever caught anything at this time of day.' But then he goes on to say, 'But because it is you who is asking, I'll drag myself out again and I'll let down the nets.'

Are there things going on for you now where it just feels as though it's about obedience? Are you still able to play your part even when feeling tired and disappointed, and circumstances don't make sense? What keeps you going when you can't see a way through, when you are exhausted, when you are discouraged? Sometimes it is just a rugged determination to be obedient.

In the story, the disciples are at the end of themselves, but their obedience paves the way for God to show up. The nets are so full that they are beginning to tear; the abundance is so great that they are yelling for help. Sometimes we are content to merely survive, but God wants us to be fruitful. We are fixed with doing things our way, but God calls us out into deeper water. We get attached and comfortable in our small world, but God invites us to play in his big world.

There is another part to this story that I missed for many years. Simon Peter is obedient, but he isn't full of faith. He goes fishing reluctantly, with no expectation. He hasn't grasped that if Jesus is asking him, he should anticipate a catch. If he were expectant, he would use more boats, as the nets are designed to be used by a fleet of fishing vessels. God wants us to be obedient, and he wants us to be obedient with faith!

I can identify with Simon Peter: 'God, I love you. I'll be obedient but I'm struggling to believe for the breakthrough, the transformation, the bit that I am not in control of.'

Back on the shore, as the adrenaline begins to dissipate, the magnitude of what has just taken place punches Simon Peter in the gut and he falls to his knees. His lack of belief exposed, he is struggling to be around Jesus, and in this very moment of weakness Jesus calls him.

Jesus declares that this is not a time to be afraid, and affirms who they are and what they have been made to do. Simon Peter's response this time shows that he has understood what is really at stake. Financially, they have just hit the jackpot with that massive catch; however, that is nothing compared to the invitation to follow Jesus. The great haul of fish and their entire livelihood is left on the shore in a symbolic and reckless faith response.

The end to our Escape and Pray adventure was far less dramatic: we left a few faithful prayers on the shore before jetting home. However, the call to follow Jesus is the same – like the early disciples, Jesus invites us to leave our small world and shallow waters and to join him on a faith-filled adventure.

'I press on toward the goal to win the prize for which God has called me heavenward in Christ Jesus.'

PHILIPPIANS 3.14

9

Calling and hope: glimpses of heaven

'Hi Rich, bit random – please would you pray for me today?'
I looked down at the text message on the phone in my hand.
I happened to be in Spain at the time, but it wasn't just my
surroundings that seemed foreign. I reread the message and
knew it was something serious.

The prayer request was from my university friend Simon,
and given that his friendship with God had drifted since
then, it was indeed random. Though we were born in the
same hospital six months apart, grew up less than five miles
from each other and attended the same sixth form college, it
wasn't until we both turned up at Loughborough University
as freshers that Simon and I would cross paths. I was
instantly glad we did – he was great company and great con-
versationally. We soon became friends and later housemates,
sharing a house in our second year at university with four
other friends. It was in this house, which provided lots of
space to sit and talk through big life questions, that Simon
started a friendship with God which, like many university
friendships, later drifted, though his belief in God never
really did.

Returning from Spain, I caught up with Simon, who
shared with me the news of his diagnosis: cancer of the

bowel that had spread to the liver. He also explained how he had reached out to God in prayer and been surprised to find that God was much closer than he had imagined. In the face of death, Simon was finding he needed an eternal perspective to make sense of the call on his life, something he knew that, through my own journey with Josiah, God had shown me a little about.

A glimpse of heaven

Sometimes it isn't enough to see our lives in our time-bound, sin-bound, glory-bound, battle-bound life on earth. We need heaven's perspective to see our lives in the light of eternity. We need this especially when we encounter life's brutalities and injustices and receive news of events from friends and strangers that are horrifyingly cruel and unfair. We need a place to turn to and a prayer on our lips that whispers, 'Come, Lord Jesus.' We need a more expansive horizon, one that reminds us that there is more than what we see around us and that, above the noise of distress, hope shouts defiantly and courageously. We need a summons that calls us upwards and announces that one day everything will be well.

This eternal perspective on our calling was something I had known in theory ever since I had given my life to Christ, but just a few short days after my son Josiah had died, I learned again just how real that promise remains.

'Sometimes it isn't enough to see our lives in our time-bound, sin-bound, glory-bound, battle-bound life on earth. We need heaven's perspective to see our lives in the light of eternity.'

Josiah was born on the Monday, he died on the Tuesday and on the Friday I had to travel from Loughborough to Leicester to register his birth and his death. This was an unusual and unwanted task, yet at the same time I was still reeling from the tragedy and appreciated the space the car journey provided. I have often valued time on my own in the car, with no music or radio on – just space to think and sometimes to pray. This journey looked set to be one of those times, and I was typically quiet and reflective.

Ten minutes in, as I reached the outskirts of Loughborough, everything changed. My car, with me in it, continued to travel towards Leicester, only I was spiritually somewhere else. I have no recollection of the journey that day, but as I arrived in the city centre, my cheeks wet with tears, I had no doubt in my mind as to what had just happened.

The Lord is close to the broken-hearted, and he came close to me that day; the atmosphere in my car became thin and I had a vision, a vision that took me by surprise and which shocked and delighted me. It didn't last very long, but long enough to awaken something deep in my spirit and enable me to glimpse life from an eternal perspective, from God's perspective.

In my mind's eye I saw Josiah in heaven. He was no longer the helpless baby I had cradled in my arms a few days earlier. Now he was standing in front of me and he was a fully grown man.

I wasn't expecting this. I believed in heaven and the resurrection of our bodies, but had no real framework for it. Heaven was a comforting idea more than a strong conviction. Yet the person I was staring at was unmistakably my son. He carried my likeness, but was better looking (not easy for a dad to admit), his eyes blue and emanating peaceful assurance, his complexion glowing, his striking dark hair tumbling down his shoulders. A man in his prime, he looked healthy and strong – a health and strength that affects me deeply to this day.

In the time I had with Josiah in intensive care, I knew that his spirit was strong. It is difficult to describe, but I sensed a strength in him that was so at odds with his condition. He was so poorly, his heart broken and kept alive by tubes, wires and the attentiveness of compassionate medical staff. Yet present in his tiny form there was such powerful, God-breathed life. He was too strong to remain in the weak and broken shell of his little body. A life that, rather than being clung to, was waiting to be released.

The apostle Paul refers to himself when he shares:

I know a man in Christ who fourteen years ago was caught up to the third heaven. Whether it was in the body or out of the body I do not know – God knows. And I know that this man – whether in the body or apart from the body I do not know, but God knows – was caught up to paradise and heard inexpressible things, things that no one is permitted to tell.
(2 Corinthians 12.2–4)

In the midst of tremendous pain, this vision was the kindness of God, as he let me take a tiny peek at what lay in store for those who love him. Bible doctrine could in no way prepare me for this encounter, this revelation. Paul, in his previous letter to the church in Corinth, declared:

'What no eye has seen,
what no ear has heard,
and what no human mind has conceived' –
the things God has prepared for those who love him –
these are the things God has revealed to us by his Spirit.
The Spirit searches all things, even the deep things of God.
(1 Corinthians 2.9–10)

I had felt over the previous few days that I had already touched and experienced some of the deep things of God. In this vision I was beholding Josiah as he had been planned in the heart of God and would be for ever. I thought back to the Tuesday afternoon when Josiah lay peacefully in our arms, and how quiet the room was. As we dedicated Josiah to God and prayed what felt like the costliest of prayers, I imagined Jesus stretching out his arms to hold him. I now understand things differently. As Josiah crossed the thin veil between death and life, it was the most tremendous home-coming. And Josiah did go straight into the everlasting arms of Jesus, not to be held as a baby but embraced as a man.

Another glimpse

This unexpected encounter in my car has been a source of much hope and has shaped me in my journey as I outwork the call of God on my life. It was to be followed by another deeply moving moment when, eight months later and still in the thick of grief, I received a letter from a lady called Helen.

Helen was a leader with a strong prophetic gift, from another part of the church in Loughborough. She gently and humbly offered me an ordinary blue envelope that contained the most extraordinary letter I have ever received. To encourage us in our calling, God will often choose to speak prophetically through people, reminding us again and again of the plans he has for us. In many ways, the dream Helen had written down rang true with the vision for a student movement I had all those years ago in a fireside chair: a field of students ready to be harvested and hired for kingdom work.

> *'To encourage us in our calling, God will often choose to speak prophetically through people, reminding us again and again of the plans he has for us.'*

These prophetic promises can provide anchors of hope and windows of perspective when life is tough and it is hard to see clearly. Here is an excerpt taken from the dream Helen shared with me. I pray that her encouragement to me would reveal something of heaven's perspective on your own calling:

I found myself walking through countryside with open fields, at harvest time. I knew I was in heaven. A tall young man approached me and I knew he was Josiah. He led me into a field full of fully ripe golden corn that was being harvested.

'This is the field my father worked in,' he said. 'Tell him that the intentions and desires of his heart and the visions of what he saw could happen are fully acceptable to God. Tell him that he is not accountable for other people's response and neglect, nor for circumstances that halted the work. Tell him about the mature, ripe harvest field that you see now. Tell him about eternal completion and that his work is judged on the basis of his willingness to be fully obedient to the vision he saw. The work he started and sweated over is now complete. Tell him that what he has done is acceptable and that it doesn't all depend on him. God brings to completion and is the author and finisher of works of faith. Abraham believed God and it was credited to him as righteousness. Tell my father that his faith caused the work to begin and that faith will complete it. His work will not complete it. God will ensure its completion, by faith. Look at me! Am I not complete? He saw me by faith, but he was not permitted to work to bring about my maturity. God has brought about my transformation in partnership with my parents' faith. In the same way, this field is a work made complete.'

I saw the same fields and countryside, but they were a picture of the present, set in time rather than eternity. I saw you in a field of unripe but ripening corn, making an appeal to heaven for more help, attention and workers. You examined the work done, assessed the incomplete work, but then, in peace and at rest, turned and left the field and closed the gate behind you.

This picture still overwhelms me. Heaven has a perspective on our calling. It isn't for us to judge its value and declare its success or failure. Heaven has different metrics, and only God does the measuring. Heaven's perspective is about your faith – how are you investing it? Are you being faithful to

God's call on your life? The writer to the Hebrews declares, 'God gave his approval to people in days of old because of their faith' (Hebrews 11.2, NLT Open Bible) and then goes on to list both the familiar and the more unlikely heroes in the Bible and how they all received God's approval, yet none of them received all that God had promised.

We sow seeds, we act in faith and we occasionally glimpse what matters most to God. Heaven sees the big picture, the trajectory of our lives; heaven joins dots we don't even know exist and aligns them with God's perfect will. We try to follow; we stumble and fall and we sense the upward call of God in Christ. Heaven cheers and applauds our every effort and sounds the trumpet, summoning us towards the prize.

> 'Heaven sees the big picture, the trajectory of our lives; heaven joins dots we don't even know exist and aligns them with God's perfect will.'

Heaven is real

Heaven's perspective on our calling changes everything. Billy Graham talked and wrote a lot about heaven, and one of his famous quotes is, 'Life is hard, but God is with us and heaven is real'.[1] It is a short sentence that packs a punch. Life is hard and is full of adversity, much of which is too great for us to handle alone. Yet we have the most faithful companion – the Spirit of God is with us and tenderly gives us all we need. Our hope, then, is not in our circumstances, but in the hope we have in Jesus. The risen Christ is in heaven, standing, praying and preparing a home for us.

'Set your sights on the realities of heaven' and 'think about the things of heaven' is how Paul exhorted the Christians in Colossae (Colossians 3.1–2). This can be difficult for the Western believer, who has so many distractions and physical comforts. Heaven, or the idea of it, can become an all-too-familiar concept but not a reality, not a hope; rather heaven becomes a place of fantasy where all our dreams come true, but we don't really believe it is a real, physical place and that we will spend eternity there.

The central theme of Jesus' teaching was the kingdom of heaven. He taught us to pray, 'Our Father in heaven' (Matthew 6.9) and left this earth to go to heaven. If it is good enough for Jesus, shouldn't we take heaven just as seriously? How can we do this?

Paul is writing to the Colossian Christians and challenging them to live up to and think on their spiritual position in Christ. He is admonishing them to focus on heaven, to daydream about heaven and to meditate on, ponder and muse on the things of heaven, and to think about the resurrected Christ and what it means for their 'real life [to be] hidden with Christ in God' (Colossians 3.3, NLT).

What we think on, meditate on and contemplate affects who we are becoming. It reflects our values and what we hold dear, and it ultimately affects how we live our lives. C. S. Lewis wrote:

If you read history you will find that the Christians who did most for the present world were precisely those who thought most of the next. It is since Christians have largely ceased to think of the other world that they have become so ineffective in this.[2]

'What we think on, meditate on and contemplate affects who we are becoming. It reflects our values and what we hold dear, and it ultimately affects how we live our lives.'

A God of justice

Of course, holding heaven in mind will not prevent pain in our lives; it will help us live in the tension as we hold on and hold out for God's promise of resurrection life. This side of heaven we won't see the justice that we long for. The justice that we see in society may mean a perpetrator ends up with a prison sentence, but this is not true justice. It is never able to fully compensate and restore to the victim what has been lost. The scales of human justice are unbalanced and broken. We feel injustice deeply, be it the result of a tragic accident or the evil actions of another person – life is unfair. We all endure the disruptive, rootless sense of alienation that is the ugly fruit of our own and other people's sin. We need God to straighten us out and save us from ourselves.

God is love, and out of his love he will set the world right. That includes you and me, the things we've done and the things done to us that have had a negative impact on our lives. God will judge the living and the dead and will restore what has been robbed, and he will give us an inheritance that won't perish, spoil or fade (see 1 Peter 1.4). Ness has always talked about this inheritance with a glint in her eye and a smile on her face. She regularly says, 'The only thing we can take with us from this world is people; people are the only thing we can take with us!' People saved by the grace of God will populate heaven and be the reward that Christ died for.

Presence and pain

We approach so much in life as if everything is clear and understandable. The physical universe is a vibrant place and our physical senses are designed to lap it up. However, we begin to look at the world differently when we feel the impact of brokenness through pain.

The world has no answer for pain. It can medicate, build castles of false comfort, look for solace in relationships and sex; it can press fingers into our ears and go into deep denial. It can't deal effectively with pain. Only God has an answer to pain and suffering, and it is twofold.

The first answer is found in God's presence. The presence of God doesn't remove the pain – at least not immediately in most instances – rather God draws near to us. It is the presence that Jesus talks about and promises in John 14 – a gift that takes away threat and fear, a gift that the world cannot give us. It is divine, it is from heaven, it is the presence of God through the Holy Spirit.

Beyond words and any answers we can articulate, the presence of God provides comfort, security, deep peace and assurance. It mysteriously seems to be most evident in those who have suffered the greatest and have been transformed by clinging to God. How else could a Holocaust survivor forgive his or her prison guard?

The second answer is hope. Specifically, hope of resurrection in a world that isn't how it was intended to be and how it one day will be. This was the confident hope and expectation of the early church and the many martyrs who defiantly and gladly laid down their lives with their eyes fixed on a greater prize. This is the Christian hope and is the next part of the journey for those who believe.

The Bible says we see reality as 'through a glass, darkly' (1 Corinthians 13.12, KJV). In other words, we don't see things clearly; we have a very distorted view of life. 'Our bodies now disappoint us, but when they are raised, they will be full of power' (1 Corinthians 15.42, NLT Open Bible). The resurrection is a full and complete liberation from sickness, infirmity, disability, aging and all the wear and tear of this pilgrimage towards heaven. It is total transformation and wholeness – physically, spiritually, sexually, emotionally and mentally. It is a daring and steadfast hope in the face of current pain and suffering. 'The eternal God is your refuge, and underneath are the everlasting arms' (Deuteronomy 33.27). This is the reality of the hope we have in Christ, the hope of resurrection. For me it has more depth and meaning now, not because of wishful thinking or a vivid imagination, but because of the tangible experience of God's presence and hope in the midst of my pain and grief.

When I think of Josiah, I now have two images. The first I have touched, held and seen physically – my helpless, precious baby son fighting for life and whom I have dearly missed growing up in our family. The other is of a man whose destiny is now assured through Christ's death and resurrection and is alive and whom I look forward to embracing one day. Both are my son. This is the very real hope we have in Christ. And it is the very hope that my old university friend Simon was experiencing as he approached the end of his earthly life.

Baptized into hope

Simon was usually smiling or laughing – mostly at a joke he had just made. We would often laugh along with him, sometimes because his joke was genuinely funny but often because his laughter was infectious and day-brightening. It was difficult not to be lifted by his presence. And though the circumstances of our post-holiday catch-ups were bleak, Simon's outlook wasn't.

Simon's relationship with God was being rekindled and it was providing a much-needed perspective on the trial he was enduring. Simon talked about facing death and dying and the hope he had in heaven, and as I listened intently, two things really stood out.

First, Simon resolutely refused to be bitter; he always had a thing about how ugly bitterness was. Not only that, he refused to feel entitled to a long life; he knew life was a gift and he had benefited from so many of life's blessings. Simon was incredibly thankful throughout his cancer journey.

Second, he knew where he was going. 'Rich, I just know when I die, I am going to a better place,' he once said to me. It was more than wishful thinking; there was a conviction in his voice and he didn't seem afraid.

Those things challenged me. In fact, Simon's honest and authentic way challenged most people who spent time with him, especially during his last 18 months: he wanted us to take a deeper look at the important things in life.

When it came to the last six months of Simon's life there was something profound going on inside him. He had managed to dodge being baptized at university and now he was desperate to be. He asked if Ness and I would baptize him. Having read up on what baptism meant, he was now impatient to be baptized, to make a public declaration to follow Jesus and to be baptized into the life and hope that he offers. Going down into the water symbolizes death and coming up out of the water symbolizes resurrection life.

He travelled to us the following Friday with a change of clothes and a towel. We waded into a beautiful part of the River Soar with him. It was August and the water wasn't cold, but as we lowered him down and pulled him up again he trembled uncontrollably. Suddenly the heavens opened, as if attuned to the significance of the occasion – the rain was as heavy as you're ever likely to see it. We stayed rooted to the riverbed for a few minutes, breathing in the holy moment, nature applauding all around us, and I have no doubt that God was smiling on him. We then sat down on the riverbank and prayed together.

Twenty-two years after we had first met, I sat down with Simon for the final time. I travelled to London specifically to sit with him during his chemotherapy and he surprised me by talking about going back to work. It would be the last time I saw him. Alongside the deep sadness at Simon leaving us so early, I had a huge sense of pride. I was incredibly proud of him because he finished his life well.

In times of suffering, sometimes we see the very best in humanity. I saw this in Simon: his attitude, his thankfulness, his awareness of others. He saw his life in terms of quality, not quantity. It takes revelation of what God has in store for those who love him to transition to that way of thinking; it is this revelation that enables us to see hope in the darkest of places.

Calling and hope

'Our hope for the future comes from the future; it comes from Christ who has gone before us and prepared a place for us, who leads us by the hand and calls us by name. When we see Christ, we see hope.'

D. L. Moody says, 'We talk about heaven being so far away. It is within speaking distance to those who belong there. Heaven is a prepared place for a prepared people.'[3] By the grace of God, Simon was prepared, and although his body was wasting away, his appetite for God was voracious and his hope unquenchable. His life read like the letter to the Corinthians:

Therefore we do not lose heart. Though outwardly we are wasting away, yet inwardly we are being renewed day by day. For our light and momentary troubles are achieving for us an eternal glory that far outweighs them all. So we fix our eyes not on what is seen, but on what is unseen, since what is seen is temporary, but what is unseen is eternal.

(2 Corinthians 4.16–18)

Until we are faced with life and death situations it is so difficult to see our calling in the light of eternity, and even when we do, that light is often dim and distorted. Once again, our hope *for* the future comes *from* the future; it comes from Christ who has gone before us and prepared a place for us, who leads us by the hand and calls us by name. When we see Christ, we see hope.

C. S. Lewis puts it beautifully when he says:

At present we are on the outside of the world, the wrong side of the door. We discern the freshness and purity of morning, but they do not make us fresh and pure. We cannot mingle with the splendours we see. But all the leaves of the New Testament are rustling with the rumour that it will not always be so. Someday, God willing, we shall get in. When human souls have become as perfect in voluntary obedience as the inanimate creation is in its lifeless obedience, then they will put on its glory, or rather that greater glory of which Nature is only the first sketch.[4]

There is a longing for more in every human being. It was a revelation to me that it is okay to have some longings that can't be satisfied this side of heaven. I don't have to go hunting around to try to fill them, and neither do you. Each of us has an ache for God and a longing for more. He has planted eternity in the human heart (Ecclesiastes 3.11). Longing doesn't need to be torturous; it keeps us on track, it stops us becoming complacent and it stops us becoming self-sufficient.

This is the message Jesus proclaimed, this is why creation is groaning and aching, this is the hope of the Church, this is the upward call of God in Christ. Life on earth, with all its beauty and battles, adventure and adversity, love and longings, dreams and disappointments, is just a glorious foreshadow of what is to come. When we say yes to the call of Christ, we enter into this sure and steadfast hope, so much so that it radically changes how we live because of who we are living for.

As we will see in the following and final chapter, because we are so fixated on the physical and material in the Western world and Church, this message of hope is far too easily lost in plain sight. Our hope is often in what we see, yet our faith is about confident expectation in God and in what we don't see.

'I press on to reach the
end of the race and receive
the heavenly prize for
which God, through Christ
Jesus, is calling us.'

PHILIPPIANS 3.14 (NLT)

10

Calling and movement: run your race

Finding a job, getting promoted, meeting a partner, getting married, buying a house, having a child, getting *another* promotion, having *another* child . . . In our comparison-rife and consumerist culture, we can all too easily equate living a life of calling with reaching as many life 'milestones' as we possibly can this side of heaven. I hope you have realized by now that the God of the Bible has a very different perspective on our calling.

The Bible talks about our calling as a race. The writer to the Hebrews declares that there is a 'race marked out for us' (Hebrews 12.1). However, our prize is not the accolades, titles and trophies we might collect during the race; it is Jesus who is the goal. The race marked out for us leads to Jesus, and only you can run your race towards that 'heavenly prize' (Philippians 3.14, NLT).

> 'As our journey with calling within *this book*
> draws to a close and your journey with calling
> outside *its pages races on, let me ask you: how*
> will you run your race?'

We don't get to choose when it starts or finishes, and it can take a while for us to realize that we are even competing.

But when that realization does dawn, we have some choices to make, habits to form and disciplines to embrace to be able to fulfil our call to run our race well. As our journey with calling *within* this book draws to a close and your journey with calling *outside* its pages races on, let me ask you: how will you run your race?

On your marks

As I have thought about running the 'race marked out' for me, I have imagined this metaphor – used seven times in the New Testament – playing out in a number of different ways. The modern Olympics is iconic for the 400-metre race track. It is easy to imagine our race being like that: we need to stay in our lane while running hard, before collapsing over the finish line, exhausted.

I have also thought of the race as a marathon, 26.2 miles of relentlessly putting one foot in front of the other, a demanding endurance race requiring mental resolve to keep going, to overcome tiredness and discomfort. In order to reach the finish line, the race must be run in a sustainable way.

I now prefer to think of the race as an obstacle course. Think Tough Mudder rather than school sports day. Tough Mudder is a ten-mile mud-and-obstacle course designed to drag you out of your comfort zone by testing your physical strength, stamina and mental grit. With no podiums, winners or clocks to race against, it's not about how fast you can cross the finish line. Rather, it is about overcoming a series of challenges that emphasize teamwork, creativity and accomplishing something *tough*. Competitors finish caked in mud, bruised and bloodied, elated and gloriously alive.

'We don't get to choose our race, the course,
the terrain, the obstacles. We do get to choose
how we run.'

What kind of race have you been called to run? It might be difficult to comprehend what running the whole of that race will look and feel like. It will almost certainly have some huge challenges along the way, probably one or two tragic events, seasons of love and loss, living with tensions and longings, and internal battles around generosity and greed. You might find yourself enduring poverty or stewarding millions, choosing daily between risk or safety, living with fear and faith. Whether you are living for yourself or for God, you can be sure the finish line is fast approaching, and that this is a race you only get to run once. We don't get to choose our race, the course, the terrain, the obstacles. We do get to choose *how* we run.

Starting well

Outside the venue was a strapping young man with a broad smile who introduced himself as Tamas. He continued, in broken English, to declare, 'Jesus, he's so good, so good!' Tamas was 19 years old and was studying at the University of Miskolc in northern Hungary. He had decided to make the 528-mile round trip to be part of a student gathering in Pécs, southern Hungary.

The reason for his almost-permanent smile became apparent. Tamas went on to share how two and a half years earlier he had been an out-of-control teenager who was ripping his own family apart. He was addicted to computer games and had been admitted to a psychiatric hospital. It was there that Jesus met him. A supernatural encounter with the risen Christ would break the chains of oppression in his life and was an ignition moment that would lead to his health, sanity and family being restored.

Tamas knew why Jesus was 'so good'. He had been rescued from a very dark place, and with his calling in Christ now awakened, he was running the race marked out for him. The ripple effect of the ignition moment created a fire that led to his parents finding Christ and staying together, and as a family starting a church for their street.

Tamas had a voracious appetite for Jesus, and his passion was dangerously infectious. Tamas had started his race well, and in the early part of our race passion for Jesus is perhaps the most important element. Passion for Jesus will get us a long way, and I don't think I have met many students or people I would describe as too passionate for Jesus! I think back to the enthusiasm of my friends when I was a student and have observed since that it can be relatively easy to start the race well or to give that impression. What I am increasingly impressed by is men and women who can keep this passion alive for the long haul, long past their student years and into their twenties, their thirties and beyond . . .

Hitting the wall

Forty. An age that once was in an unimaginable future had now arrived and was soon to pass as a distant memory. This might be hard for you to believe, but I was really look-ing forward to turning 40, probably more so than I had looked forward to any previous birthday. I had a strong sense that much of my life up until that point had been training for what was to come. I was keen to build on what I had learned, discovered and dealt with and to leave some of the hard seasons, competitiveness and comparison of the previous years behind. As I approached 40, I had a deeper and more profound sense of calling than ever before: my goals and declarations for the coming decade were clear and simple, representing the three main areas of calling in my race around being a husband, a father and a leader. But something wasn't quite right.

It was around this time I began to notice some discomfort in my chest. Quickly, the noticing turned to focusing and the focusing turned to obsessing and the obsessing was filling my mind with fears. I was unaware of what was happening. I was feeling sensations in my chest and body that were becoming deeply unpleasant and frightening. My mental template for serious illness had been affected by recent events with family and friends and I found myself having dark thoughts about my own health and well-being.

I visited the doctor and had tests to monitor my heart and health that revealed nothing, yet still the discomfort and fears persisted. Three weeks after my fortieth birthday I was away with friends and felt scarily out of control, despite my best efforts to hold it together. Whenever I was still, I felt a buzzing in my body that stopped me from sleeping. I'd go to the toilet four or five times in the night, my appetite was diminishing, my chest felt as if it had spiders crawling inside it and I couldn't take deep breaths. This went on for seven days. I was sleep deprived and terrified. I thought something was seriously wrong with me; I thought I was going to die.

My race had hit a wall. Many marathon runners describe hitting a wall around the 18-mile mark. The muscle glycogen levels are depleted, but it is the brain that effectively puts the brakes on in an act of self-preservation.

As dramatic as this season might sound, I have since discovered that such experiences are common to many of us at some point in our lives. If you personally haven't had to battle with anxiety or some sort of mental health challenge, I am sure someone close to you has. The good news about hitting a wall is that it doesn't signal the end of your race; it does mean that there are some more life lessons to learn and pay attention to – lessons that have the potential to deepen calling, help you run your race better and lead you into greater freedom.

Back home and tearful, I visited the doctor again. He gently explained to me that it was the body's fight or flight response to fear that had led to me experiencing considerable stress and anxiety. The doctor prescribed me some medication and said the excess adrenaline in my body needed to be burnt off with strenuous exercise. He was very confident that I would recover, but said it would take six to nine months for my body to recalibrate. I was shocked; I hadn't seen this coming. Ness and my close friends were equally surprised. My life at that time was not particularly stressful and I have a relaxed and laid-back personality. What was going on?

As soon as I returned from the doctor's surgery, I dug out an old pair of running shoes and attempted my first three-mile run in a long, long time. I then proceeded to run three miles every day for the next 30 days to burn off the adrenaline. It was physical discipline, but also spiritual. It hurt like hell, but it was the start of another transformative journey, one that would reveal more about the race I was running and those I was running alongside. With each stride I prayed, pressing into warfare with an enemy who so often wants to steer us off course.

Subtle lies

Why was I so full of fear about my health? I took this to God in prayer and he reminded me of a moment a few months earlier when I had climbed up a small hill and felt a twinge in my chest. God reminded me of the thought I had had in that moment: 'This could be serious.' The thought was a lie that stuck in my heart and mind like a barbed fish hook. Unwittingly, I had believed a lie about my health and allowed it to be given ground in my life.

Behind every besetting fear there is a lie, and this lie was the source of my fear. It was a moment of revelation and I felt incredibly relieved as well as a little bit stupid. The enemy doesn't have many tricks and I had entertained one of his bluntest and most direct strategies. I turned to God, renounced the lie and repented of my fear. In Christ, these sorts of fears are easy to deal with, although staying free requires spiritual and physical discipline, friends and courage.

Another lie we can too easily operate under in our individualistic age is that we must be strong; that to ask for help is a sign of weakness. As I get older, I realize I am more fragile and broken than I would ever have admitted as a young man. This brokenness, rather than something to be ashamed of, has become a holy comfort. It is in the very areas of weakness and brokenness that I find Christ. My best efforts to fix myself are no match for the grace and mercy of God.

If this resonates with your journey, I have great news: God charts a course for our healing, and as we learn to surrender our brokenness to Christ, he guides us into greater peace with ourselves and with the world around us.

Even though we are running to a 'heavenly prize' (Philippians 3.14), we are running in our earthly bodies – broken, bruised and brilliantly in tune with where we are spiritually and emotionally. Our bodies are often an accurate barometer for how we are doing. Throughout this time of anxiety around my health, I was also getting an insight into my body's response to stress. Life events catch up with us all and our bodies remember things in a way our minds forget. I'd dealt with the fear, but I was still getting weird sensations in my chest. I wanted to bring God right into the heart of my physical journey, and I sensed that some of the emotional trauma from my thirties was being carried in my body and it needed to find a way out. Instead of fighting the sensations, I needed to learn to welcome them, trusting that they weren't hostile or a threat.

Emotional pain in our lives, whether from childhood or from the previous year, often needs to find a physical escape route. You and I are fearfully and wonderfully made, and our emotional, mental, physical and spiritual parts are knitted together in such a way that one affects the others. Only with God can we face our own inner world with honesty and courage.

Fear

*'Fear always creates barriers to the full life
Jesus promises us; we need to push back.'*

This lie around my health caused me much fear. Lies always do. And if we are not careful, fear can grow and grow, causing a significant roadblock to how we run our race. I don't know about you, but my fears consistently jeopardize my ability to see hope and they limit my freedom. The fears we experience as we seek to live out our calling are wide and varied, although the common ones are around fear of death or dying, fear of never having enough, fear of being alone, fear of being unloved or abandoned. These specific fears often reveal some core beliefs and lies: that deep down we don't believe heaven is real, or that how we live matters or whether God loves us. Fear always creates barriers to the full life Jesus promises us; we need to push back.

One of the core fears we can experience in the Christian life is the fear of not having enough. The Bible tells us to 'not store up for yourselves treasures on earth . . . But store up for yourselves treasures in heaven' (Matthew 6.19–20). And yet, through fear and greed and pain and mistrust, it is all too easy to be distracted from our 'heavenly prize' and be drawn to the earthly prizes that can sometimes appear much more tangible in the here and now. In other words, fear of not having enough can invite materialism into our hearts, weighing us down in our race towards Christ. I know I can like my stuff too much: gadgets, phone, house, car, computer, clothes, the list goes on. They become 'things' from which I subtly and sometimes explicitly derive comfort. You may even find yourself buying stuff to comfort you, rather than seeking out God who provides comfort now and in doing so gives you a foretaste of your future comfort in heaven. It is so important for us to run towards God for our comfort and satisfaction, 'for where [our] treasure is, there [our] heart will be also' (Matthew 6.21).

In our search for earthly comfort, we can also fall into

the trap of being too satisfied now. This is especially true in life's summer seasons when we're tempted to switch off from the urgency and compassion Christ feels about the world. I can prefer the foretaste of heaven available here on earth. C. S. Lewis puts this pertinently: 'Has this world been so kind to you that you should leave with regret? There are better things ahead than any we leave behind.'[1] What fears do you need to face in order to run your race better?

Comparison

Another stumbling block in our race towards our 'heavenly prize' is closely linked with the fear of not having enough, and it's a killer in our social-media-driven culture: comparison. When we surrender our lives and calling to God, we can trust that God will shape, mould and develop us in ways that fit with who we are so that we can make our best contribution in life. And yet, it can be so easy for us to want to fit into someone else's mould. The stories of the rich, young and famous fill news columns, but they are also the rare minority. There is nothing wrong with being inspired by others, but don't compare. Young millionaires, footballers, YouTubers, musicians and actors – indeed, most celebrities – are not realistic role models. Embrace the ordinary steps in front of you and allow God to do the extraordinary with you. God wants to give you kingdom dreams and visions, not pipe dreams and fantasy.

I love this advice from Galatians 6.4 (NLT): 'Pay careful attention to your own work, for then you will get the satisfaction of a job well done, and you won't need to compare yourself to anyone else.' Comparison is crippling to growth and personal development, whether we feel better or worse – it is not the measure God has for us. Jesus gives short change to Peter's request in John 21.22 when he enquires about the future fate of another disciple: 'If I want him to remain alive until I return, what is that to you? As for you, follow me.' In short, concentrate on *your* calling, not on anyone else's.

The more I have reflected on the short phrase 'the race *marked out for us*', the more convinced I am that in Christ we each have *our own* race to run. None of the 'life milestones' that I listed at the beginning of this chapter are guaranteed, and if you find yourself 'left behind', you are not – you are just running a different race. This phrase states the obvious that we often fail to see. When we think about calling, it is all too easy for our first thought to be about other people and what they are doing with their lives and how they are running their race. Looking at the runner next to us will increase our chance of running out of our own lane and may even disqualify us from the prize. How other people have run their race is to serve only as an inspiration or a warning, not a comparison.

> *'The more I have reflected on the short phrase "the race* marked out for us*", the more convinced I am that in Christ we have* our own *race to run.'*

Expanding horizons

Subtle lies, fears, materialism and comparison can all cause us to stumble as we run our race, and I have noticed that the temptation to settle for a more comfortable, more risk-averse life has intensified since I turned 40. This is at odds with the lifelong faith adventure we are called to. A truly satisfying and fulfilled life can only be found in active pursuit of Christ, and sometimes we need to actively combat the things that get in the way. That is exactly what I was seeking to do and model when I took my then 12-year-old daughter, Amelie, on a dad–daughter adventure to India.

Ness and I had agreed on the trip a few years before with the rationale that this was a formative time in Amelie's life and it would be good to expose her to life outside the West. We wanted her to experience and get to know people living in poverty first hand, to see and taste other cultures, to witness other religions and to appreciate what she had in her life. Most of all, I wanted to spend some quality time with her before she became a teenager. I hoped that this would help her run the teenage years well and with a larger life perspective.

In India, Amelie and I travelled around with my good friend David and his 12-year-old daughter, Mia. I'd known David for 15 years, ever since he'd been a student worker in Belfast, and now he and his family had been living in India for four years. Our trip came together with just six weeks of planning and involved time in slums and cities, schools and charities, beaches and jungles, as well as in the homes and lives of local people. One of the most memorable moments was going on a short jungle trek just outside the perimeter fence of where we were staying for a couple of nights. The fence was designed to keep the larger animals, such as elephants, tigers and leopards, outside this rural jungle retreat.

Our guide that day was Manu. He was an expert in tracking

and once in the jungle he gave a short talk on the dangers that wild elephants pose to humans. He chose a poignant place to share this information, as we were standing by a recently knocked-down teak tree that a young bull elephant had dismantled and shredded all the bark off. Manu went on to share that these elephants are particularly dangerous, and if we were to find ourselves in the same vicinity we were to jump into the 12-foot trench that runs through the jungle and lie down, as this would prevent the elephant from reaching in with his trunk, picking us up and then trampling us to death! This was unlike any nature walk Amelie and I had ever been on.

Our senses heightened thanks to Manu's pep talk, we picked our way through the damp jungle with Manu pointing out animal tracks and plant species. The walk was exhilarating. Then Manu suddenly stopped, raised his hand and placed his finger on his lips. There was a seriousness in his eyes and he gestured to us to smell by cupping his thumb and forefinger to his nostrils. Quietly he asked if we could smell the musty, manure-like aroma. We could. Nostrils flared, eyes scanning the dense undergrowth and rooted to the spot, we held our breath. It wasn't fresh elephant's dung that we were smelling; it was the elephant's tongue. We were smelling the elephant's breath, and we were in danger.

Danger has a smell

I have to admit that in that moment there was a part of me that wanted to see the elephant, curiosity overriding the warning signs. I was tempted to flirt with danger. The smell was subtle, but the danger was real. Paul in his letter to the Galatians observes, 'You were running the race so well. Who has held you back from following the truth?' (Galatians 5.7, NLT).

Eugene Peterson translates it as, 'You were running superbly! Who cut in on you, deflecting you from the true course of obedience? This detour doesn't come from the One who called you into the race in the first place' (Galatians 5.7–8, MSG). This is often the way with temptations – they are subtle and can present as harmless, or even fun. However, anything that would hold us back from our calling is a danger. Most temptations don't lead straight into a life-or-death situation; however, if succumbed to habitually they become like iron shackles around our legs and can stop us running altogether. What starts with a bad choice can end in pornography, drugs, gambling, sex addiction, relational or marital breakdown and being a million miles from the fullness of life that Christ has for us.

Thankfully, Manu didn't waiver in his opinion: we needed to retreat, and do so hastily. As we outwork our calling in God and look to run well, we must also be attuned to danger. What currently threatens your race? Where might you be tempted to veer away from your true course? What small choices could lead to addictive habits? Just like our physical senses, we need to trust our spiritual senses – our discernment. If it doesn't smell quite right it is time to stop, reflect and pray, and where necessary run away fast in the opposite direction. The writer of Proverbs puts it bluntly: 'Don't even think about it; don't go that way. Turn away and keep moving' (Proverbs 4.15, NLT).

The exhortation to run the race marked out for us sits in one of the most illuminating parts of Scripture. Hebrews 11 is all about faith in God and tells of the great men and women who were commended for their faith and whose reward is caught up with our race:

> Therefore, since we are surrounded by such a great cloud of witnesses, let us throw off everything that hinders and the sin that so easily entangles. And let us run with perseverance the race marked out for us, fixing our eyes on Jesus, the pioneer and perfecter of faith. For the joy set before him he endured the cross, scorning its shame, and sat down at the right hand of the throne of God. Consider him who endured such opposition from sinners, so that you will not grow weary and lose heart. (Hebrews 12.1–3)

I imagine this great cloud of witnesses on their feet, leaning forward on the tips of their toes, urging us onwards with dramatic hand gestures and making a deafening roar as they shout encouragement. They are willing us to cast off anything and everything that would hinder our race and, because of their vantage point, they can see more of what is at stake in our lives. Heaven is on our side. F. F. Bruce notes, 'It is not so much they who look at us as we who look to them – for encouragement.'[2] The passage is clear: we are to join this long line of faithful people and run in a way that is consistent with their faith.

Disciplines of kindness

The start of my forties felt like an initiation into the second half of life and, by the grace of God, led me to form new habits that would help me run better in the decades to come.

Discipline has never come naturally to me, but over the years I have learned to love it. In my twenties, discipline was like relating to an awkward uncle that I didn't really get on with. In recent years, discipline has become more like a close friend: I don't need it to survive, but I do need it to thrive. Henri Nouwen describes discipline beautifully:

> But when discipline keeps us faithful, we slowly begin to sense that something so deep, so mysterious, and so creative is happening here and now that we are drawn toward it – not by our impulses but by the Holy Spirit. In our inner displacement, we experience the presence of the compassionate God.[3]

Discipline is about looking after yourself; it is about being kind to yourself. It is through discipline that you can not only see your calling get off to a good start but also see it lead to a life of fruitfulness and fullness. How do we pace ourselves when we don't know the length of the race? Disciplines help us pace ourselves and stay true to our course.

'It is through discipline that you can not only see your calling get off to a good start but also see it lead to a life of fruitfulness and fullness.'

The great news for our race is that we don't need any special gear or fancy watches that measure our heart rate, calories and steps. The race we are called to run isn't dependent on having money and resources, it isn't engaged through being given opportunity or responsibility, nor is it in any way connected to status, titles or popularity. None of these things matters for our race, as our race is primarily about the habits and disciplines that shape our inner life and adventure. The one who calls us to run holds the starting pistol and the finishing tape and promises to give us everything we need to run well. The apostle Paul writes to the church in Corinth:

> Don't you realize that in a race everyone runs, but only one person gets the prize? So run to win! All athletes are disciplined in their training. They do it to win a prize that will fade away, but we do it for an eternal prize. So I run with purpose in every step. I am not just shadow-boxing. I discipline my body like an athlete, training it to do what it should.
> (1 Corinthians 9.24–27, NLT)

Discipline is also the way to participate in our own healing. As we have seen, our society and our dislike of discomfort mean we celebrate and look for quick fixes – a paracetamol to cure a headache, more pills and tablets to combat depression and anxiety. We pray prayers for instant relief and miraculous intervention. All of these have their place. However, healing is often a process. A cold takes a few days, a broken bone six weeks, ligament damage could be six months. We love to know how long in order to be back in control.

Into what areas are we inviting God that are beyond our control? In what areas can only God heal us? In what areas is God inviting us to participate for our own healing? What disciplines do we need to embrace that will lead us into greater freedom? For many of us, our training will require:

- the discipline of giving and developing generosity to heal us of self-sufficiency;
- the discipline of complimenting and speaking well of others to heal us of pride;
- the discipline of sharing our homes and possessions to heal us of materialism and individualism;
- the discipline of pursuing deep friendships to heal us of loneliness, independence and isolation;
- the discipline of grieving to heal us of emotional loss;
- the discipline of gratitude to heal us of envy and comparison.

The list goes on and on, and you can add your own.

Choosing well

Our wholeness and freedom to 'run the race marked out for us' is connected to our holiness. Some of the fears, lies and anxieties we battle can be traced directly to how we are choosing to live. We can participate in our own healing by going to bed at a regular time and getting enough sleep, by limiting our screen usage and understanding the impact of what we watch, by eating healthily and exercising regularly, by working hard and doing things that replenish us. All this requires discipline, and discipline is being kind towards your current and future self. All these are forms of discipline that affect our spiritual and physical lives alongside the familiar ones that Dallas Willard describes:

We can become like Christ – by following the overall style of life he chose for himself. If we have faith in Christ, we must believe he knew how to live. What activities did Jesus practice? Such things as solitude and silence, prayer, simple and sacrificial living, intense study and meditation upon God's Word and God's ways, and service to others. Some of them will certainly be even more necessary to us than they were to him, because of our greater or different need.[4]

We don't pursue holiness, discipline and training in order to discover our calling; we do so because God has and is calling us. It is a response to the call of God that will enable us to run our race with joy and perseverance not only for our student years or our twenties and thirties, but for the long haul.

Wherever you are in your race and however you have run the race up until now, whether you have been chasing after the wrong things, made some really bad choices or even been mown down by a few elephants, you have an opportunity to run well in the next season of life. In the same way that lies and fears can start small and snowball, so can the disciplines we create in cultivating a race that will withstand all that comes against us.

Start where you are, start small, start with a few mumbled prayers. Choose to put one foot in front of the other, choose to invite a trusted friend on the journey, choose to run the race marked out for you.

Summary
Called by God

You fling wide your curtains in the morning and the sunrise floods in. The intense light startles the photoreceptor cells in your eyes and summons your body to awareness. Of all the light wavelengths, the morning orange light has the greatest impact for resetting the body clock and dispelling weariness. A burst of orange light boosts brain activity and cognition and stirs the body to greater alertness and action. I hope that, as you have been reading the book in your hands, you have sensed a new day in your calling, God's light has arrested your senses and illuminated how loved you are, and a deeper sense of calling has been awakened in you.

The question that remains is: how will you move forward? From the stories I have shared and as you reflect on your own life in a new light, we can agree that what happens in our lives doesn't define our calling, but our calling in Christ defines us and gives our lives meaning. Wherever you are, God knows, and you are primarily called to pursue friendship with God.

> *'The question that remains is: how will you*
> *move forward?'*

God has designed a plan and purpose for your life that is as unique as you are. You may be aware of what this is or you may still be figuring it out, and I hope you know that is okay. The most important thing is to keep moving forward. Over the years I've found myself in many conversations of quiet desperation with finalists and graduates who have a mild sense of dread about what their next step is and how to take it. If you feel stuck, the next step can feel like the most important and defining decision that you have to get right. It isn't and you don't. Our calling happens as we move, and so taking a step to keep moving is what is needed. However risky it feels, however blind the step, however little you understand or see how it will pan out or how it fits with who you are – it doesn't matter as much as you imagine. Remember you have a Guide who is committed to leading you into a fulfilling and fruitful life and in a direction where that can happen. And if you dare to look and keep looking, straining sore eyes and blinking back tiredness, I can guarantee you will discover God's calling for your life.

I recently had a picture in my mind while I was praying that reminded me of Isaiah 43.19:

For I am about to do something new.
See, I have already begun! Do you not see it?
I will make a pathway through the wilderness.
I will create rivers in the dry wasteland.
(Isaiah 43.19, NLT)

In the picture I saw a river flowing through wasteland and barren places. Wherever it went, the land would awaken and come to life. Ahead of the river the colours were bland and muted, but where the river touched the earth there was an explosion of life, vibrancy and colour. What was unusual about this picture was that the river was not made up of water; it was made up of people. People who carried the life of God and whom God was charging and calling to work with him to bring about transformation. People who were so full of the life of God that when their feet touched the ground it brought new life and energy to the neighbourhood.

I felt God grabbing my attention and revealing more of his heart again. First, he highlighted that as we pray for a move of God, that move is going to happen as we participate with God in his work. Our prayers for revival will lead to action and proclamation. Second, God doesn't want us to be ignorant to the power of the Holy Spirit in our lives. When we go with God, we can expect things to change both in us and around us.

God wants to do something new in you! It has already started. Do you recognize it? As calling is awakened in you it can feel uncomfortable and create inner tensions. When we experience this, it is important not to rush to conclusions but to keep trusting and moving. God is passionate that his movement should become your movement and that you move in the direction in which he is moving.

> 'Only with God's calling will your life make sense. What's more, it is worth the effort, worth investing every ounce of strength, worth more than anything you will ever own materially.'

The movement of God is creative, beautiful, purposeful and transformative; there is enough for each of us to join in with and to find meaningful and fulfilled calling. There is no one size that fits all, only some common denominators that revolve around seeking first God's kingdom and loving our neighbours. To pursue the call of God is to enter into a wide and liberating space, full of beauty, purpose and potential. Teeming with life and creativity, it is gloriously alive. Only with God's calling will your life make sense. What's more, it is worth the effort, worth investing every ounce of strength, worth more than anything you will ever own materially. Order your life around that call: it is who you were made to be.

Father God,
Awaken me to your calling.
I want to follow and respond to your call.
I ask for forgiveness for when I have chosen muddy paths and my own way.
I now choose your way.
Thank you that you are calling me by name.
Take my hand and lead me in the fullness of life that Jesus promises.

Fill me with your Holy Spirit for the adventure ahead;
do something new in me.
Amen.

Study guide for small groups and further reflection

It is likely that you have come to this book with questions, and the reading of it may well raise many more. It can be helpful to journey through these questions intentionally, whether by journalling alone with God or by grappling with them out loud with friends or a small group. I hope that in exploring these questions they will help provoke daring prayers and meaningful conversations.

For each chapter, reread the main content, reflect on the key verses listed below and then prayerfully journey through the questions, asking God to reveal his will for you as you do. At both the beginning and the end of your explorations, remember God's question is paramount: 'Ayeka?' – Where are you in relation to him?

1 Calling and you: hearing the call

Key scripture
1 Samuel 3.1–19

Key quotes
We can't escape the fact that our childhood shapes us. The lessons learned in these early years are often hidden and subconscious, only to surface in later life. For many of us, they provide hints of our calling integrated into who God has made us to be.

This is the paradox of calling: you are called fully and completely today and at the same time God's calling grows in you and shapes how you live moving forward.

Self-discovery takes time, and you may need to give yourself a break and be kinder to yourself as you wrestle with longings whose times haven't yet come.

Questions
- Calling is often rooted in us from the beginning. What can you identify from your childhood that has a connection to your calling?
- What else has God woven within you? What are your desires? Your skill sets? What do you enjoy doing? When was the last time you made a decision to go somewhere new or acted on an instinct?
- Many of us fall into the trap of thinking we are too 'ordinary' to be used by God. Are there any excuses you are making that are getting in the way of pursuing your calling?

- What can you learn from Samuel about how he responded to God's call?
- Often our unique calling needs time to cultivate, and it's good to start where we are: are there places you need to visit? Are there people you need to pursue and hang out with as you help to identify the unique calling God has put on your life?

Prayer

Lord God, help me to be like Samuel, to learn to recognize your voice and respond to your call.

Amen.

2 Calling and character: longings and seasons

Key scriptures

Psalm 131; Psalm 26.2; Ecclesiastes 3.1–14

Key quotes

You might be able to identify with similar 'sticky thoughts' – questions and dreams that refuse to let go and keep hanging around, inviting you to muse on them.

Calling almost always involves stepping outside our comfort zone and into some big unknowns. God's calling on our lives is always for something bigger than ourselves.

Calling tends to be incubated in ordinary places, tested in dark places and realized in unlikely places.

Each season can offer a picture of what may be going on spiritually in our lives.

Questions

- Have you experienced any 'sticky thoughts'? Or are you still waiting for them to come? Do you have a yearning for something bigger than yourself?
- Calling isn't a place at which you will arrive; it is being cultivated right now wherever you are. Which season are you in now, and why?
- Waiting in life is inevitable. What do you feel you are waiting for right now? How have you actively engaged in your 'waiting'? How can you make the most of this season?

- Where has your calling been tested? Is God inviting you to take any risks?
- Have you had to lay down any dream, or do you have a sense that God is asking you to?

Prayer

Lord God, help me to wait patiently for you, to learn what you are teaching me in the place where I am and to trust your timing for the things you are calling me to.
Amen.

3 Calling and community: dangerous firebrands

Key scripture

Acts 2.42–47

Key quotes

The holiness that God has for us is personal, corporate and social, and that means we find tremendous freedom in being with friends where we can be fearlessly honest, daringly vulnerable and ruthlessly accountable.

In the age of social media and a culture that celebrates being liked by a multitude of acquaintances, it can be easy to mistake followers for friends. But God, who lives in community as Father, Son and Spirit, has hardwired us to be intimately known and has designed us to work out our calling in community.

A rigorous discipleship culture through the asking of questions that helped men and women pursue God's calling.

Questions

- Who is your community?
- How would you like that community to develop?
- What can you do to help build that kind of community – real, authentic, offline community?
- What questions do you need faithful friends to ask you regularly to help you pursue God's calling?
- Think of the things God may be calling out from within you. Who out of the community of believers

that have gone before can you learn from? Whose legacy can you build upon?

Prayer

Lord God, thank you that you have welcomed me into your community. Help me do the same for others, encouraging them in their calling and welcoming their help as I pursue mine.

Amen.

4 Calling and pain: a long, dark night

Key scriptures

Isaiah 53.3; John 11.1–38; Isaiah 45.3

Key quotes

All suffering causes grief. A loss of a loved one; a loss of a dream, a job, an identity, a friendship; a loss of control of some kind. The only way to move through suffering is to grieve, and it is fair to say that most of us aren't very good at grieving. We are good at feeling sorry for ourselves, but that isn't grieving. Often our pain is suppressed or compartmentalized, but the problem with unprocessed pain is that it leaks.

We bear a scar which in time becomes a story of God's grace that can comfort and strengthen others. Our pain, when transformed, becomes a gift to give away.

How we respond to God in these times strengthens or weakens our sense of calling and determines and shapes our destiny. Heaven has a different perspective on our trials and tribulations, and by God's grace we can glimpse and embrace it.

In every community of people there are things to celebrate wildly and things to mourn deeply going on at the same time.

Questions

- When have you suffered in life? How have you found God in that suffering?

- Where do you still need healing? Do you believe that God's healing is greater than your brokenness?
- Can you begin to see a link between your pain and disappointments and parts of your calling?
- What treasure have you got to give away?
- Romans 12:15 exhorts us: 'Rejoice with those who rejoice; mourn with those who mourn.' How easy do you find doing this? Who can you celebrate with today? Who can you mourn with today?

Prayer

Lord God, thank you that you are close to the broken hearted. Come close to the broken parts of me and help me surrender them to you.

Amen.

5 Calling and money: hustling with faith

Key scriptures

Matthew 6.19–33; Matthew 7.9–11; Acts 20.35

Key quotes

Alongside calling is often a sense of lack. We can't do it on our own; we haven't the talent, skills, resources or people.

Money is a resource to bless and enable our calling, and God wants us to have a healthy relationship with it.

What would it look like to choose abundance over scarcity? How would that affect your life and your calling? Life to the full in God has an abundance of love, joy, peace, patience, kindness, goodness, faithfulness, gentleness and self-control (Galatians 5.22, NLT), so why do they seem so scarce? Money is finite, but these attributes know no limits.

'In fundraising we discover that we are all poor and that we are all rich, and in ministering to each other – each from the riches that he or she possesses – we work together to build the Kingdom of God.'

Questions

- Do you live in awe of God's abundance or are you all too aware of what you lack? What would it look like to choose abundance and how would it shape your calling?
- Where have you experienced God's provision in your life?

- When have you taken financial 'risks'?
- How do you feel about asking for money? How do you feel about being asked to share your money?
- Who and what are you giving money to and why?

Prayer

Lord God, help me to trust you with money and to put your kingdom first, confident that you will provide everything I need for the life you have called me to.

Amen.

6 Calling and battles: I will stand

Key scriptures

Psalm 23; Psalm 26.12; Luke 15.11–24

Key quotes

He calls us close and invites us to share what we'd struggle to say to others or even to find the words to vocalize at all. Lovingly and gently he asks, 'Where are you?' And before we have time to reply he makes room at his table and beckons us to be with him.

The outworking of my calling to church and students felt like it was being continually disrupted, but in reality my calling was being deepened. I regularly found myself like the lost son – I had nothing to offer; I just needed the embrace of the Father. That was enough for God and slowly I was learning that was enough for me too.

The seasons where we feel weak and vulnerable are rarely times to make big decisions.

I became aware that I was wearing labels like lanyards . . . Hanging around my neck, they were beginning to define me and even get in the way of both my freedom and my calling.

Questions

- What are the enemies in your life at the moment? Have you brought them into God's presence? What is God's perspective?

- Where have you had to make a stand? How did you do that?
- How kind have you been to yourself recently?
- The lost son came home assuming an identity that didn't fit with how his father saw him. Are you aware of any labels that subtly or otherwise are part of your identity? Do you see yourself as a victim? If so, how? What do you need to do to take those labels off?

Prayer

Lord God, I want to take my stand in you and for you. Help me to agree with you about who you say I am.
Amen.

7 Calling and perseverance: grace and grit

Key scriptures

Psalm 37.23–24; Jeremiah 6.16; 2 Corinthians 4.16–18

Key quotes

Slowing to a walk can also help us detect God's perspective on our lives and the way we are walking. Most importantly perhaps, it affords us the time to question whether we are walking in step with him. It takes time to learn how to walk with God.

What else keeps you going? What keeps you putting one foot in front of the other through life's ups and downs? Our walk needs to be full of purpose, and that purpose is fuelled by godly ambition.

In our fast-moving culture, it can be all too easy to overlook where God has us now in favour of where we want him to take us.

With God nothing is too dark, too broken or too far gone. With God there is always a way, and he will walk with us down that path.

Questions

- Consider the road you are on. Will this road lead you into all that God has for you? Do you feel you are walking in pace with God?
- What else keeps you going? What keeps you putting one foot in front of the other through life's ups and downs?

- Have you ever considered that the people you are now serving and the places where you are now working are a doorway to your calling? What else does God want to teach you right where you are?

Prayer

Lord God, I want to walk in step with you. Help me to keep moving at your pace and to trust that your call on my life is on track and headed in the right direction.

Amen.

8 Calling and adventure: Escape and Pray

Key scriptures

John 2.1–11; Luke 5.1–11

Key quotes

The outer adventure without the inner adventure will very likely lead to empty hedonism. It is the inner adventure that gives the outer adventure roots and context. The inner adventure is our pursuit after God.

Start the detox now. Turn off notifications, remove social media apps, even lock your phone in a drawer, unsubscribe from Netflix, and allow your body and mind to breathe again. Reclaim your imagination and creativity; it has been quietly suffocating in the name of entertainment.

If we had to do it over again, we would reflect more.
If we had to do it over again, we would risk more.
If we had to do it over again, we would do more things that would live on after we are dead.

Sometimes we are content to merely survive, but God wants us to be fruitful. We are fixed with doing things our way, but God calls us out into deeper water. We get attached and comfortable in our small world, but God invites us to play in his big world.

Questions

- How do you filter what you consume? What would a healthier media diet look and feel like?

- When was the last time you did something adventurous?
- If you could live your life over again, what would you do differently?
- Do you recognize the moments when you are fully alive? Does that affect what you give your time to?

Prayer

Lord God, thank you that life with you is an adventure. Help me delve into the inner adventure, and give me courage and conviction to embrace the outer adventure.

Amen.

9 Calling and hope: glimpses of heaven

Key scriptures

1 Corinthians 2.9–10; Colossians 3.1–3; Philippians 3.14

Key quotes

We need heaven's perspective to see our lives in the light of eternity. We need this especially when we encounter life's brutalities and injustices and receive news of events from friends and strangers that are horrifyingly cruel and unfair.

To encourage us in our calling, God will often choose to speak prophetically through people, reminding us again and again of the plans he has for us.

Heaven has a perspective on our calling. It isn't for us to judge its value and declare its success or failure. Heaven has different metrics, and only God does the measuring.

What we think on, meditate on and contemplate affects who we are becoming. It reflects our values and what we hold dear, and it ultimately affects how we live our lives.

Questions

- What do you think about when you think about heaven? How do you set your sights on heaven?
- Heaven has a different perspective on our current circumstances and our calling. What are you currently dealing with that could be seen differently from heaven's perspective?

- Have you ever received any prophetic words about your calling? Is there someone you could ask to pray with you about this?
- Are the things you are thinking about and meditating on in line with a heavenly perspective?

Prayer

Lord God, there are times when the glass I am looking through is especially dark. Help me to see both my circumstances and my calling from your perspective.

Amen.

10 Calling and movement: run your race

Key scriptures

Galatians 5.7; Hebrews 12.1–3; 1 Corinthians 9.24–27;
Philippians 3.14

Key quotes

The good news about hitting a wall is that it doesn't
signal the end of your race; it does mean that there are
some more life lessons to learn and pay attention to.

God charts a course for our healing, and as we learn to
surrender our brokenness to Christ, he guides us into
greater peace with ourselves and with the world around
us.

This is often the way with temptations – they are subtle
and can present as harmless, or even fun. However,
anything that would hold us back from our calling is
a danger.

Discipline is about looking after yourself; it is about
being kind to yourself. It is through discipline that you
can not only see your calling get off to a good start but
also see it lead to a life of fruitfulness and fullness.

Questions

- How are you running your race? Have you set your
  sights on the right prize?
- What currently threatens your race? Where might you
  be tempted to veer away from your true course? What
  small choices could lead you into danger?

- What disciplines can you embrace that will help you run better? What patterns will help you run well, not just for the moment, but for the long haul?
- Who can help you in running your race well? Can you make a commitment to speaking and praying with that person regularly?

Prayer

Lord God, I really want to run my race well. Fill me with your Holy Spirit so I will have all the perseverance and endurance I need to outwork your call on my life.

Amen.

About Fusion

Fusion exists to see students find hope in Jesus and home in the local church. It is a movement that serves more than 2,500 churches across many nations. It trains and resources student workers and catalyses student small groups. <www.fusionmovement.org>

Notes

2 Calling and character: longings and seasons

1 Parker J. Palmer, edited by Henry F. French, *40 Day Journey with Parker J. Palmer* (Minneapolis: Augsburg Books, 2008), p. 74.

3 Calling and community: dangerous firebrands

1 Dorothy Sayers, 'The Whimsical Christian', *The Greatest Drama Ever Staged* (New York: Collier Books, 1978), p. 14.

2 Roger Forster, 'The Fusion Conference: A History of Student Mission', Derby, England, November 2000.

3 Eugene Peterson, cited in Gerald L. Sittser, *Water from a Deep Well* (Downers Grove: IVP, 2007), p. 10.

4 John Foxe, *Foxe's Book of Martyrs* (Whitaker), p. 309.

5 Roger Forster, 'The Fusion Conference'.

6 John Wesley, Journal, 24 May 1738, *Works*, 18:249–50.

4 Calling and pain: a long, dark night

1 C. S. Lewis, *A Grief Observed* (London: Faber and Faber, 1961), p. 1.

2 Chinua Achebe, *Arrow of God* (London: Heinemann, 1964), p. 84.

3 Eugene H. Peterson, *A Long Obedience in the Same Direction: Discipleship in an Instant Society* (London: IVP, 2000), p. 54.

5 Calling and money: hustling with faith

1 Augustine of Hippo, *City of God*.

2 Parker J. Palmer, edited by Henry F. French, *40 Day Journey with Parker J. Palmer* (Minneapolis: Augsburg Books, 2008), p. 34.

3 'Take the First Step in Faith. You Don't Have to See the Whole Staircase, Just Take the First Step', <https://quoteinvestigator.com/2019/04/18/staircase/>.

4 Henri J. M. Nouwen, *A Spirituality of Fundraising* (Nashville: Upper Room Books, 2010), p. 49.

6 Calling and battles: I will stand

1 Frederick Buechner, *Whistling in the Dark: A Doubter's Dictionary* (New York: Harper Collins, 1993), p. 84.

2 Godfrey Birtill, 'After I've Done Everything (I Will Stand)', 2007. Used with permission.

3 Anthea Lipsett, 'Christian Group to Take University to Court', *The Guardian*, 27 July 2007, <www.theguardian.com/education/2007/jul/27/highereducation.uk2>.

4 Os Guinness, *No God but God: Breaking with the Idols of Our Age* (Chicago: Moody Press, 1995), p. 13.

7 Calling and perseverance: grace and grit

1 Student Linkup is a resource that helps prepare students for life and university and has connected tens of thousands of students to churches in their place of study through a mobile app. See <www.fusionmovement.org/studentlinkup>.

2 Jim Forest, *The Road to Emmaus: Pilgrimage as a Way of Life* (New York: Orbis Books, 2007), p. 9.

3 Eugene H. Peterson, *A Long Obedience in the Same Direction: Discipleship in an Instant Society* (London: IVP, 2000), p. 166.

4 Henri J. M. Nouwen, *A Spirituality of Living* (Nashville: Upper Room Books, 2011), p. 27.

8 Calling and adventure: Escape and Pray

1 Between 2015 and 2017, more than 200 teams were sent by Fusion

to different European university cities to Escape and Pray, on a mission to pray for the university, connect with the church and be ready to be used by God. See <www.fusionmovement.org/adventure>.

2 'How Children Lost the Right to Roam in Four Generations', *Daily Mail*, 15 June 2007, <www.dailymail.co.uk/news/article-462091/How-children-lost-right-roam-generations.html>.

3 A. W. Tozer, *The Knowledge of the Holy* (New York: HarperCollins, 1961), p. 1.

4 'Life in man is the glory of God; the life of man is the vision of God' (Saint Irenaeus of Lyons).

5 Sir Ken Robinson, 'Do Schools Kill Creativity?', TED Talks, February 2006, <www.ted.com/talks/ken_robinson_says_schools _kill_creativity?utm_campaign=tedspread&utm_medium= referral&utm_source=tedcomshare>.

6 Stuart J. H. Biddle, 'Physical Activity and Mental Health in Children and Adolescents: A Review of Reviews', NCBI, September 2011, <www.ncbi.nlm.nih.gov/pubmed/21807669>.

7 Heard in a sermon.

8 Jim Forest, *The Road to Emmaus: Pilgrimage as a Way of Life* (New York: Orbis Books, 2007), p. 144.

9 'Health at a Glance 2015', OECD, <http://dx.doi.org/10.1787/health_glance-2015-en>.

10 John Helliwell, Richard Layard and Jeffrey Sachs (eds), 'World Happiness Report 2017', <http://worldhappiness.report/ed/2017/>.

11 Gunnar Gunnarsson, 'Europe's Most Godless Country May Surprise You', The Gospel Coalition, 4 March 2017, <www.thegospelcoalition.org/article/europes-most-godless-country-may-surpise-you>.

9 Calling and hope: glimpses of heaven

1 Billy Graham, *The Journey* (Nashville: Thomas Nelson, 2006), p. 308.

2 C. S. Lewis, *Mere Christianity* (San Francisco: HarperSanFrancisco, Harper edition, 2001), p. 134.

3 D. L. Moody, *The Way to God and How to Find it* (New York: Fleming H. Revell Company, 1884).

4 C. S. Lewis, *The Weight of Glory and Other Addresses* (Grand Rapids: Eerdmans, 1949), p. 13.

10 Calling and movement: run your race

1 C. S. Lewis, 'Letter from Lewis to Mary Willis Shelburne, 17 June 1963', in Walter Hooper (ed.), *Collected Letters, Vol III: Narnia, Cambridge and Joy 1950–1963* (London: HarperCollins Entertainment, 2006), pp. 1430–1.

2 F. F. Bruce, *The Epistle of Hebrews* (Grand Rapids: Wm B Eerdmans Publishing, 1990), p. 346.

3 Henri Nouwen, *Compassion* (London: Darton, Longman & Todd Ltd, 1982), p. 107.

4 Dallas Willard, *The Spirit of the Disciplines: Understanding How God Changes Lives* (New York: Harper & Row, 1989), p. ix.

Acknowledgements

It is humbling to take a moment to reflect on how my story is woven into the lives and stories of so many others. My thanks, therefore, are directed to a large number of people for enriching my journey and shaping the story I've been able to write. Some are people whose path I have crossed for only a single day, others over decades and others only through their story being told.

I am full of gratitude for the patient love of my parents, John and Lis Wilson, and the wider Wilson family; they gave me a start in life I am deeply grateful for. Their prayers and availability have fuelled and facilitated Ness and me to respond wholeheartedly to the call of God in our lives. Our wider household over the years has included many others, and to those who have shared our home and our table, every interaction and conversation leaves a trace. It may well be that you can hear your words in what I have written; thank you.

My time and friendships at university set a course for my life, and led to me immersing myself in the wonderful community known as Open Heaven – it is this community that has embodied and shaped so much of the thinking and theology behind the stories I have told. This lived experience of shared life in Christ has formed and transformed what has been written. Thank you, Open Heaven.

To the Fusion team, you have my respect and admiration for continually making bold and courageous choices in responding to God's calling; your passion fuels my passion. Thanks for all the encouragement you have given me during the writing of this book and for taking the time to read and comment; both I myself and this book are better because of your faithfulness.

Alongside the Fusion team are the generations of students, student workers, church leaders and board members who have joined in the work of Fusion to see students find hope in Jesus and home in the local church. As new waves of salvation are breaking across the universities, your obedience to God's calling will see many respond to God. Some of the student mission stories I've told are thanks to you and the best are yet to come.

Writing a book requires expert input and I have had that in abundance from Elizabeth Neep and the SPCK team. Thanks for the encouragement, challenge and advice, and for your prayerful reading and rereading of the many drafts.

Words are not enough to express my love and thanks to Ness, for supporting me in sharing some of the most defining and painful moments of our life together, and to Amelie and Lauren – this is our story and I am so proud of you all.

Copyright acknowledgements